Live well as you live but

DON'T DIE BEFORE YOU DIE

| BINU VARGHESE |

BLUEROSE PUBLISHERS
India | U.K.

Copyright © Mr Binu Varghese 2024

All rights reserved by author. No part of this publication may be reproduced, stored in a retrieval system or transmitted in any form or by any means, electronic, mechanical, photocopying, recording or otherwise, without the prior permission of the author. Although every precaution has been taken to verify the accuracy of the information contained herein, the publisher assumes no responsibility for any errors or omissions. No liability is assumed for damages that may result from the use of information contained within.

BlueRose Publishers takes no responsibility for any damages, losses, or liabilities that may arise from the use or misuse of the information, products, or services provided in this publication.

For permissions requests or inquiries regarding this publication, please contact:

BLUEROSE PUBLISHERS
www.BlueRoseONE.com
info@bluerosepublishers.com
+91 8882 898 898
+4407342408967

ISBN: 978-93-5741-002-1

Cover design: Muskan Sachdeva
Typesetting: Rohit

First Edition: February 2024

Live Great as You Live, but..

DON'T DIE BEFORE YOU DIE !

Preface

It has been a great inspiration to reach out to People – Blowing into the Bugle, speaking out, being realistic more out of personal experience & knowledge gained, by being present out there, not confined to Meeting rooms and the Office. As a Public Speaker from my younger days in School, this would be normal practice. Yet, writing a Book & getting it Published – is not normal practice for a small-town person. Yet, here it is!!

This is not an Autobiography from Binu Varghese. I will leave that for Nelson Mandela's inspirational ' Long Walk to Freedom ' and the revered 'Experiments with Truth' by Mahatma Gandhi. This is about my life- a 'probable' showcase to Youngsters, Young Adults, and People who have sky-rocketed high in life, have come crashing down, and still kept walking. Walking ahead, actually!

My Million thanks to People who have continued to hold my hands, inspired me, motivated me, and still keep such a close relationship, that I am not going to DIE BEFORE I have a Medical Certificate that I AM DEAD! Not able to take names here, as my very supportive Publishers are demanding another Book if I must take each of those names! Each of my Soul Mates / Mentors / Classmates from 34 years ago, the groups I have been engaged with, and My Wonderful, Loving, Caring Dear Family! Each one mentioned above- knows who I am talking about, in every Chapter as you read along.

Let's Keep Walking.

Mr. Binu Varghese.

binuddbud@gmail.com

People Development Consultant, School Captain, Best Aloysian Student, Global Senior Management Corporate Professional Career, ICF Certified People Development Life Coach, Mentor, Business

Consultant, Public Speaker, Trainer, Motivational Speaker, Change Management Consultant, Basketball Player, National Gold Medal Winner- Debating, National Executive – Nehru Bal Sangh, NGO Navchetana Founder, collapsed at the Bangalore Airport, awaiting to Board a Flight to London, medically 'sort of' diagnosed with ...Okay... Okay... Not an Autobiography, as I remembered!

Foreword

It's truly my proud privilege and I am honored to pen a few sentences for this wonderful book of my soulmate Binu Varghese.

Memories remain unfaded from our school days when we both were in the youth movement- YCS/YSM. We had the golden opportunity to represent our Country in the 'World Youth Day Celebration' at Santiago – de Compostela (Spain) in 1989 and Denver (North America) in 1993.

All through I found a true friend in Binu. Highly focused, his abilities, talents, intelligence, prudence, and wittiness always amazed me. His concern for parents, love towards family, and responsibility towards society made him an adorable person. He was and still is, the nucleus of our group.

Binu soared to the limitless in his professional career and accomplished everything within his reach. But the vicious attack of the rare autoimmune disease 'Neuro Sarcoidosis' made a standstill in his life.

I am happy that he is overcoming the challenges with new priorities and missions. He is now a Life Coach and Founder President of 'THE SUCCESS STATION' People Development Consultancy - 'Mentoring, Training, and Career Counsellor'.

I am happy that he is back with the Youth, being a beacon of light for them.

A born fighter Binu Varghese is living through in and throughout in this book "DON'T DIE BEFORE YOU DIE." The pages of this book are a message to many who surrender themselves to life's uncertainties and live complaining about their lives.

Each line will reveal the words of Dr. APJ Abdul Kalam -

"Look at the sky. We are not alone. The whole universe is friendly to us and conspires only to give the best to those who dream and work"

Dr. Prof. Annsi Sojan Joseph
Professor In Education –
Christ College, Bhopal

EACH LESSON LEARNT, IS A LESSON LEARNT!

(Read that line once again)

Contents

1. Embracing the Beautiful Threads of Life: A Journey from Birth to Accepting One's Roots............ 1
2. What happened, Binu?... 5
3. Chapter 3... 7
4. A Journey of Uncertainty 8
5. Roots of Joyful Bonds 20
6. Growing up to be a leader and Picking My Own Path ...31
7. The Guiding Light of St. Aloysius...............................47
8. Understanding Life Outside of the Classroom 53
9. Inspiring Spirituality and bowing to the Divine. 60
10. Stepping into Success 64
11. Being open to growth and change................................70
12. Finding Your Way Through the Medication Maze 77
13. The Power of Positivity 83
14. Handrails and Lifelines: 92
15. Embracing Roots, Reconnecting, and Living with Sarcoidosis 100
16. Winning Over Difficulties 107
17. Dealing with Problems and Accepting Them 118
18. A CEO's Wisdom: Embracing Change for Growth 125
19. Learning to Accept Change..134
20. Defying the Shadows 142
21. Make Peace with the Rebel inside you.......................150
22. Inspiration comes from Anywhere- 157
23. Accepting the Challenges of Life...............................160
24. Refusing to Die Until I Die.......................................166
25. Walking Your Path to Purpose..................................173

Chapter 1
Embracing the Beautiful Threads of Life: A Journey from Birth to Accepting One's Roots

December 24th was the day I breathed air for the first time in this wide world. Friends still joke, "Oh, just one day more, and you would have shared your birthday with Christmas, the grand celebration!" The laughing tones reverberated, meaning that I almost had my birthday on the day of global celebration.

But imagine me, Binu Varghese, battling for attention with the grandeur of Christmas. Trying to steal the spotlight on the same day as the miraculous conception of our Lord Jesus Christ? A giggle and a "Huh!" greeted the idea.

I took comfort in the idea of having a special day all to myself, even if it wasn't a day that existed anywhere else in the world. A special day that was commemorated everywhere from homes and neighborhoods to classrooms and campuses to the bustling workplace. As it happened later, the corporate world took me by storm, yet I was able to stay connected to my hometown of Jabalpur, Madhya Pradesh, India.

My journey through life has helped me recognise my special place in the world and the lives of people around me. It wasn't a private room, but it had an air of exclusivity that made me feel special. My travels have taken me through the ups and downs of life, from the hectic halls of a major Global Corporate; to the peaceful town where I was born.

There's a special alchemy that happens when you find your place in the world and make it your own. It's like a tapestry, with each event, emotion, and relationship serving as a thread. As my adventure progressed, I was able to add yet another detail to the tapestry that was my life.

Oh, the feelings that tinged my travels! Memories of schoolyard hilarity, friendships that survived the perils of puberty, and relationships cemented in the fires of small-town Jabalpur. These were the yarns that knit together my life and made me seem so cozy.

In the enormous landscape of international business life, I became entangled in the unrelenting chase of success. My days became woven together with goals and deadlines. But even amid all that chaos, there were times when I was reminded of the value of human connection.

One of the most touching things that has ever happened to me is, when I walked into my Office, on time as usual. It was my Birthday and I expected everyone in my Office Team to remember the Managing Director's Birthday despite how busy they were. A simple "Happy Birthday" and a warm smile was all that I was prepared for. However, it was amusing when I walked in and people did the usual "Hi, Good Morning Sir". I walked into my office cabin and was exhilarated that my Office was all decked up with Balloons, Ribbons, and Posters signed by each employee, wishing me a very Happy Birthday. Next to my Chair, stood a smiling Office Secretary, Sunita Nair wishing me a Happy Birthday with a hug. Then the whole team walked into the Office and burst out into Singing "Happy Birthday to you". It was an incredible Birthday, that I remember every year since. Despite the stress of impending deadlines, I felt recognised and appreciated at that moment. It was a reminder that amidst the craziness of corporate life, there are moments of humanity that span the gap between cubicles and link hearts.

However, we always seem to come full circle in life. My medical circumstances forced me to get back to Jabalpur, the starting point of my travels.

Coming back to the place I was born, was an emotional high point of my life. Like an old friend, the sights, sounds, and scents of the site where I took my first steps greeted me warmly when I returned. It was a voyage not simply over geographical landscapes but through the halls of memory.

My steps through Jabalpur's streets carried with them echoes of my youth. The laughter of playing children, the perfume of street food wafting through the air, and the comforting embrace of familiar faces - it was a symphony of memories. In such moments, I felt a tremendous connection to the essence of who I am, rooted in the soil of my birthplace.

Moving from Bangalore and London's fast pace to Jabalpur's relative calm, was like hitting the pause button, giving me time to think. It was here that I committed to the creed of "Living well while I live but refusing to die before I die." The bustle of life was not confined to the conference rooms and meetings but could be heard in the chatter of the street markets, the playgrounds that I played in, and the reminiscences of long-lost acquaintances.

There is something profoundly beautiful about returning to one's origins and reclaiming the many facets of one's personality that are so easily lost in the quest for material achievement. As I visited loved ones in Jabalpur, I was reminded that the best occasions for celebration are those spent with those closest to you, rather than in the spotlight of public acclaim. I felt complete as the day drew to a close and I sat by the 'Marble Rocks' (Bheda ghat) and the Narmada River that had held my fondest childhood memories. The transition from the hectic corporate world to the peaceful simplicity of Jabalpur had not only molded me but also revealed the innermost emotional layers that are the foundation of my very being.

All the ups and downs, loves and losses, and memories that make up a life are colors just waiting to be applied. From the day I almost was going to be a Christmas baby to the day I found my spirit in my birthplace again, my life is a tribute to the complex beauty of this canvas.

Threads of connection, echoes of laughter, and the comfort of home are all things I will take with me as I continue to write the next chapter of my life. Birthdays may come and go, but the emotional tapestries weaved with the threads of lived events, remain a timeless masterpiece, a tribute to a life well-lived. This is why I try to enjoy the unfolding symphony of life by making the most of each day, feeling, and relationship.

Chapter 2
What happened, Binu?

Coming to the point, why am writing this book, and why It's named as it is.

"On a routine official trip to London, my life took a sudden turn at Bangalore Airport. Collapsing without warning, I was thrust into a medical mystery—Sarcoidosis. A dire prognosis of three to six months to live became the haunting backdrop of my days. Yet, amid the regimented routine of medications and medical consultations, a strange sense of liberation emerged. Supported by family, friends, and colleagues, I celebrated life's simple joys and defied the predetermined fate. Global interventions, from London to Dubai, added layers to the unfolding narrative, blurring the lines of medical certainties. As the days turned into weeks and months, the enigma of life's fragility became a tale of resilience, and the uncharted territories of the human spirit. Beyond the initial prognosis, the question lingered—what lies ahead in the unwritten chapters of my extraordinary journey? The answer remained suspended, a mystery propelling me into the unknown." The only statement remembered was "YOU HAVE THREE TO SIX MONTHS TO LIVE"

Chapter 3

You still expect to read more? You do think that I have more to tell you? Medically prescribed as " YOU HAVE THREE TO SIX MONTHS MORE TO LIVE".

Yes, I do have more to share. Much more than anybody, or even me, expected to do so.

The SIX MONTHS to live was FOUR YEARS ago !!! A medically confused community and very amused close friends dominated my landscape, as I resumed my thriving lifestyle and stepped into niche areas of life in Jabalpur- more devoted to being there for others, young adults who were growing up, assisting in shaping their careers, Training Groups and Organisation's for people development, Change Management and Development of alternative Leaderships. Even went back to School in St. Aloysius, this time not as a student, but as an ex-student, nopes, as an Ex-School Captain, no again, this time as a Globally experienced Corporate Leader- actually conducting Training Programs for Students and Oh-my- God, even Training Teachers. I didn't call it " Teachers Training"- they are already Trained which is why they are Teachers who shape lives, just as it was done for me. So, I still call it " Teacher's Interaction Workshops". Teachers also need to be updated, more with what is expected from their students as they take the next steps of life, graduating out of School. It is also an opportunity for teachers to speak out about the challenges that they have, of their own. A very demanding profession- personal lives intermingled with professional responsibilities.

Chapter 4
A Journey of Uncertainty

Come along as I take you back in time to a moment in my life when everything was changing at a breakneck pace. The story starts on a typical day, with a scheduled regular flight to London that takes an unexpected turn at the busy Bangalore Airport.

Imagine me, curling up in a corner with a good book, lost in its pages. As I immersed myself in the story, everything else around me seemed to recede. But then it happened—like a lightning strike on a sunny day—and I gave up. I had no foreboding signs, no cues to prepare myself, just a sudden blackout. The atmosphere, which had before been characterised by light chatter, now resounded with the weight of serious worry.

Passengers, who had only just been strangers on the same trip, became my lifelines as I lay there, limboed between the worlds of awareness and sleep. My unexpected collapse sent shockwaves across the room, and everyone's gasp for fear filled the space. In those delicate times, the softer side of humanity shone through. All of a sudden, the previously emotionless people around me became a tapestry of compassion.

Priya, the responsible person of this unexpected paragraph in my life, enters the picture. The Airline staff wasted no time in tracking her down; their records had documentation that she had done my Booking, and official Travel administrative staff, who made travel arrangements. With a mix of astonishment and determination, my ever-efficient office secretary accepted the news. She struggled under the burden of responsibility as her mind raced with a thousand thoughts. Concerns about the individual and the precariousness of a life were more pressing than the usual work travel logistics.

Urgently, Priya contacted medical help, coordinated with the airport personnel, and informed my relevant colleagues, navigating through a maze of concerns. The emotional stakes rose with each word exchanged, and each call was like a thread weaving a safety net beneath me. Her once-cold, professional demeanor suddenly carried the warmth and concern of a friend worried about a loved one. This was at 3.00 am – Morning.

A tremendous feeling of interconnectedness and vulnerability engulfed us all amidst the mayhem. As a reminder that in the vast tapestry of existence, every person and every emotion is carefully interwoven into the fabric of our shared humanity, the unpredictable nature of life has exposed the delicate strands that bind us.

Three o'clock in the morning, a lonely hour shrouded in darkness, was ruthlessly struck by the clock. My reliable office secretary Priya was suddenly faced with an incident that required her to act with extraordinary haste. She knew that every second was precious since her heart was racing in time with the clock. She set off into the darkness of night on a mission, a mission to have me transferred to the sanctuary of Bangalore's St. John's Hospital as soon as possible.

Throughout early Morning and the day that followed, my office team's frantic footfall reverberated through the hospital halls. Coworkers who were previously just staff, are now bound together by a surprising turn of events. At that very moment, it didn't matter if I was the managing director or not; I was just another cog in the wheel of a shared concern.

The air was charged with an orchestra of unspoken emotions, a cacophony of anxiety and perplexion. Uncertainty filled the air as their eyes, normally used to numbers and reports, mirrored it. The enormity of the event stunned everyone into stillness. They hesitated, not knowing how to connect the dots between formality and the unpredictability of real life. You would have seen/ heard about medical incidents before and you would understand the complexities involved- sometimes- a few times.

A thick mist of tension descended from the antiseptic halls of the hospital. As a united front, the squad debated whether or not to contact my loved ones. An unresolved mystery hung in the air, a fragile thread just waiting to be inserted into the story. At that time, the delicate boundary between one's professional responsibility and their capacity for empathy became hazy.

The burden of the unknown settled on Sunita Nair, the figure in this well-choreographed mayhem. As part of my Office assistance team, very close to me, Sunita took up the responsibility. She was at the crossroads of a major decision, having meticulously addressed office things. Without a plan for unexpected situations like these, the whole team looked for what should be done.

A kaleidoscope of feelings, including dread, anxiety, and an unspoken bond, emerged as the evening progressed. Our once-confined contacts now span the entire hospital, breaking down the barriers of traditional office spaces and professions. Amidst the stillness of the night, the team struggled with the details of a medical emergency and the delicate balancing act of being both vulnerable and responsible.

As my doctors set off on an examination journey to unravel the mystery of my unexpected fall, the hands of the clock spun mercilessly. Their scowled expressions matched the medical enigma playing out in the hospital's clinical setting. Urgently, they dove into the intricacies of my illness, intent on explaining the unexplainable... "unexplainable", I say that, again.

There was an underlying sense of worry in the quiet hallways of the hospital. Normally prepared with solutions, the medical team was now confronted with the unsettling lack of symptoms. A perplexing collapse into unconsciousness; no warning signals; no telltale symptoms. The anxious pace of the medical staff reflected the weight of uncertainty in the air.

As a patient in the intensive care unit, I lay there oblivious to the medical drama going on all around me, caught in a dreamlike state. As my lifeless body lay there, a silent witness to the dogged search for answers, the hospital room's sterile aroma surrounded me. Uncertainty is symphonised by the mechanical lullabies murmured by the machines.

With their stethoscopes and unwavering resolve, the doctors performed a battery of tests. They looked for hints that wouldn't materialize using their eyes, which are skilled at reading body language. Just the lingering reverberation of an unexpected tumble; no vertigo or migraines whatsoever. My medical file was like a canvas; with each test, a new stroke added to the complex picture of a riddle that appeared to resist reasoning.

When I stirred and opened my eyes, I was in the bed, looking around as to where I was. A round of queries from Dr. Thomas Mathew and unexpected responses from Binu Varghese. "How are you, Binu? I am okay, Sir. Am I in a hospital? Yes, you fell ill at the airport. 'Oh', a clouded mind responded.

"Binu, do you take any medicines regularly? Any Health challenges that you have?

'No Doctor, I am good. No Medicines- nothing regular anyway'.

"Binu, do you have any addictions? Smoking, Alcohol? I didn't hear the word "Drugs". Amusingly, today is when I think of that query.

Dr. Mathew said – "Binu am a doctor, you need to tell me the facts, such that we conduct treatment accordingly".

" No Addictions, Sir"

" Living in a Global Corporate world, with Meetings and Western travels, parties and cock tale breaks? Impossible!"

Dr. Thomas called up my Office and asked Sunita if what Binu was saying is the truth. We need that information for medical diagnosis".

I don't know if Sunita was smiling when she told him - "Yes Doctor, Binu has an Addiction. He has 10 to 15 cups of Coffee every day. He insists on the coffee being strong and with Sugar."

Sunita, Coffee, and YOU are part of my life even today! Coffee in smaller doses and you in ....

Even today, January 2024, I walk into the Jabalpur Indian Coffee House, and the staff, good pals by now, don't ask what would I like to order! They just get it to the table- however, only...only two to three limited edition cups, as of today. Strong Filter Coffee and with Sugar.

Stepping back, the atmosphere in the intensive care unit was electric with emotion as the medical staff conferred in hushed tones. The doctors' feelings of powerlessness due to a lack of immediate answers were a mix of frustration and empathy. For them, it was an exposed moment that served as a reminder that even in the medical field, there are enigmas that no one can fully explain.

Emotions were raging like a mild storm in the stillness of that hospital room. There was a shared worry about my stability, that went beyond the medical setting of the hospital. Loving caregivers in the truest sense, the doctors balanced their clinical training with the unprocessed feelings that come with facing the unknown. We were all able to find common ground in the face of medical ambiguity and hope because of the personal factors that surfaced.

A rock of commitment in our office, Sunita became a guardian angel when the unexpected happened. She hurried to my home, a refuge that suddenly held anxiety and bewilderment, with the burden of duty pressing down on her shoulders. As they faced an unknown future together, she kindly and resolutely took on the duty of transporting my son Aayush and wife Smita to the hospital.

The chaos within the hospital was reflected in the weather outside. The once-charged air now bore the heavy scent of doubt, replacing the usual hum of daily activity. Sunita led Aayush and Anju through the immaculate halls, her heart heaving with worry as they ventured into the unknown with each step.

My Son Aayush held on to a glimmer of optimism, his expressionless face a canvas of bewilderment and wondering what was going on. He found comfort in the familiar—his mother Smita's comforting presence—amidst the confusing medical surroundings.

The lines between their personal and professional lives began to dissolve the moment they stepped into the hospital room. The immaculate walls bore evidence to the melding of responsibilities - Sunita, my coworker, now a reassuring guide for my family. Responsibilities, empathy, and an unwritten understanding that went beyond formal positions were all interwoven strands in the tapestry.

The medical enigmas remained inside the hospital room, casting a shadow of uncertainty over what was ahead. The doctors' creased brows betrayed their careful and hopeful disposition. What lay ahead remained an unsaid question. A heavy fog of uncertainty enveloped everyone, from medical experts to family members, and placed a pall over their features. The emotional burden of the situation was too much around the place. In the unspoken covenant of solidarity faced with the unknown, eyes met eyes, reflecting a shared concern. At that instant, the walls between our professional and private lives came tumbling down, exposing the essence of our common humanity: the ability to rely on one another during periods of extreme uncertainty.

Each day in the antiseptic intensive care unit was punctuated by the buzz of equipment and the muttered chatter of medical staff as time slipped away. After what seemed like an eternity, a shift in perspective transported me to a different setting: a room flooded with natural light and ornamented with the presence of a committed medical staff. The air was heavy with apprehension, despite the fact that it was a sanctuary.

Word of the Managing Director's condition spread unexpectedly across continents as it made its way through the hospital's halls. The profound information was conveyed to Mr. Cathal Duffy, the Global CEO, to a distant location of London. He felt a growing sense of duty as his emotions overcame the physical separation. The news had become an individual rallying cry.

A guiding light of kindness, Mr. Duffy had a prominent role in the company's hierarchy. His involvement was a genuine reaction to a colleague's vulnerability, not merely an executive decision. Human nature's strands are entwined with the inflexibility of institutional frameworks. He coordinated the support equipment from across the ocean to make sure I had access to the best medical resources.

The news of Mr. Cathal Duffy's intervention brought much-needed relief to my family. It was uplifting because it showed that people were still there, even in the face of massive corporate systems. Amid the precarious equilibrium between known and unknown, acts of empathy provided much-needed support. At that precise moment, the confines of the hospital room seemed to dissolve. A tale of perseverance, optimism, and the lasting impact of human connection may emerge from the deeds of any one person—whether they were a close relative, a coworker, or even a faraway CEO.

Dear Reader, it is the people to people, connect, that I am talking about. Stop for a moment and reflect a bit about what Binu is talking about here... typing here. Speaking to himself and you too.

The diagnostic process was like navigating a labyrinth; at every step, I was led further into my history by medical papers and extensive health exams. With each step leading to either enlightenment or additional confusion, venturing into the unknown is an inherently difficult endeavor. A profound truth resounded in the calm nooks of thought amid all the chaos.

"When we don't know what to do, we don't know what to do." Read that last line once again.

My health was depicted in intricate detail in the medical records, which read like arcane codes. With each new test came more confusion and clarity as one progressed through the complex labyrinth. The atmosphere in the room grew heavier with expectation, a tangible nervousness that reflected the unpredictability of the path that lay before. Once a regular part of life, medical exams have evolved into a series of emotional litmus tests. The clinical accuracy of examinations and the icy touch of stethoscopes blended with the comforting embrace of mutual care. The diagnosing maze was a test of emotional fortitude as much as it was of physical strength at those delicate minutes

There were vulnerable moments of reflection in the middle of the labyrinth. The customary certainties of life were overshadowed by the uncertainty of what lay ahead. "When we don't know what to do, we don't know what to do" became an acceptance mantra, a soft recognition of the emotional toll that the uncertainty may take, a profound reality.

Emotions served as a compass in the middle of the maze, when the walls of diagnosis appeared impenetrable. Although challenging at times, the journey ultimately served as a reminder of the power that comes from facing uncertainty head-on and being vulnerable enough to admit when you don't know everything. Emotions entwined in the clinical hallways, linking the dots of dread, hope, and perseverance to traverse the unknown, as the diagnosing maze unveiled not only a medical story but a profoundly personal one.

Finally, Ladies and Gentlemen, the long-awaited diagnosis was revealed: SARCOIDOSIS. Binu is a special person, so there was a Bonus offer included – today's common marketing Tag- line: 1 + 1 !! It was just not Sarcoidiosis but a value-added "Neuro Sarcoidosis", This unanticipated side effect of the discovery, cast a shadow over the already complex medical landscape.

My bewildered state caused my consciousness to dance like a flickering flame. As I tried to make sense of my diagnosis, everything around me became hazy. The medical saga's protagonist was sarcoidosis, a word forever associated with mystery. The clinical walls resounded with the revelation's emotional overtones, where anxiety and doubt were intermingled. Am most certainly sort of sure, that I have added the word – SARCOIDIOSIS to your dictionary by now !!! Till now, am sure that the usual, simple – "Anti Immunity", was part of your vocabulary.

The trip, now defined by the regularity of shuttles between hospitals, reflected the internal turmoil. Whether it was from the sacred halls of AIIMS in Delhi to the specialized care of a hospital in Dubai, with each move came the silent prayer for stability and the hope for answers. Beyond the literal distance, the emotional terrain of these journeys embraced the indomitable human spirit and its capacity to persevere.

St. John's in Bangalore, the rock in this stormy sea of medical exploration, was my final destination on this adventure. Moving back here was more than just changing locations; it was reuniting with loved ones, hearing the familiar sounds of nature, and knowing that St. John's will be there to support you.

Sarcoidosis and neuro-sarcoidosis were entangled, creating a story of perseverance. I waded through a maze of emotions, aware but bruised, coping with the unknown with the steadfast love and support of my loved ones, my healthcare providers, and the safe havens that hospitals became. The diagnosis was more than simply a medical designation; it was a turning point in the story of triumph over adversity, a demonstration of the unwavering determination that persists even when confronted with unexpected medical challenges. Binu was still Breathing.

Dr. Thomas Mathew was a welcoming presence amid all the confusion, providing answers to the many concerns that had been swirling around. While seated for a heart-to-heart, his remarks sliced through the room, delivering a revelation that sent everyone to their knees. "Binu, your immunity levels are impacted by this sickness. It is not uncommon for patients with this illness to have a LIFE EXPECTANCY OF THREE TO SIX MONTHS". Those comments had an effect that lasted, putting a pall over the delicate fabric of time.

Dr. Thomas, who was often reassuring, now had the awkward responsibility of expressing the harsh truth. Once alive with the sound of medical machinery, the room was now throbbing with the seriousness of his remarks. Going beyond the clinical, it delved into the emotional feelings of mortality and the precariousness of existence.

A patient and a caring guide had a moving conversation that began as an attempt to alleviate the patient's anxiety but turned into a more introspective exchange. The emotional terrain changed as the physician spoke. All of the people in my life there, whose expressions had been somber before, now carried the burden of an exposed vulnerability. What had been measured in regular pulses suddenly unfurled as a limited, valuable resource: time. Time itself became a window of opportunity to face the transient character of existence and to seize the bonds that bound us.

Following the disclosure, the room transformed into a haven for feelings. Despite the grim diagnosis, Dr. Thomas extended more than simply his medical knowledge; his compassionate expression conveyed his willingness to lend a helping hand. Although heavy with the seriousness of the situation, the heart-to-heart conversation set in motion a path that would be characterized less by the passage of time and more by the strength that comes from being human and the unfaltering encouragement of individuals who were willing to face death head-on with one another. The Words of Dr. Thomas resonate even today. " Binu, you are being discharged today. You can go home.

Binu, stick to the prescribed medicines every day, not a single dose to be missed.

That is 21 Tablets /Syrup et all, including... err...err 14 Steroids every day. Not a single dose to be missed, divided Morning, Noon and Night.

Binu, you will not drive yourself. Anywhere you are, YOU WILL NOT DRIVE. That includes your Car and your Bike too."

I didn't ask if the Bicycle was still my friend.

Today, I learn, it is not!

At a highly emotional period, Dr. Thomas comforted them by emphasizing their steadfast support. His comments hung thick in the air as I left the hospital; six months, a timescale that had to be proven medically, now seemed like an interminable fog.

Getting back home, discharged from the Hospital, my devoted chauffeur Kumar, drove me in my Skoda, where I relaxed in the comforts of my own vehicle. Driving in my trusty old vehicle was like escaping into a fortress, providing a little respite from the unforgiving world outside. But all the while I was behind those four walls, a deluge of thoughts ran through my head. Is that six months? Not merely a length of time, but a finite period that tests the fundamental nature of existence.

The path that had been so comfortable to me previously now seemed clouded with mystery. The medical verdict was like an invisible burden, changing the course of my life with its weight. A vehicle traversing the material world, the automobile also became a vessel bearing the psychological burden of an adventure into the unknown.

With the wheels spinning beneath me, the passing landscape became a background for contemplation. There was a reverberation in my heart from the passage of six months. Like a silent storm developing inside, the emotional seriousness of the situation sunk in. Managing one's emotions in the face of a medically unknown prognosis was the real obstacle.

A trip of unknowns had just started, and with it, emotions were whirling around like leaves caught in a storm. Amid the car's isolation, the medical verdict's weight and hope's fragility met. Both the physical landscape and the psychological reverberations of the future were mirrored in the rearview mirror.

It was at that very second when the Skoda transformed from a mere means of transportation into a symbol of perseverance. With unwavering devotion and deep introspection, it transformed into a vessel that could traverse the emotional and physical challenges of a voyage when time seemed to stand still at every turn.

I confirm that most of the above text is not what I exactly remember. My good old Colleague and soulmate, Sunita Nair, recounts most of these details and my family adds to this.

"Born into simplicity, Parents born and brought up in rural Kerala, my childhood was filled with the vibrant tapestry of simple living, active pursuits, ambition, and pride instilled by my parents. Memories of cycle rickshaw rides to school, spirited games on the makeshift playfield, and the camaraderie of childhood friends painted a nostalgic picture. Fast forward to adulthood, and the unexpected reunion after 44 years brought together childhood companions, now married with families. The Indian Coffee House in Sadar, Jabalpur, witnessed the rekindling of bonds, with introductions, hugs, and smiles. The commitment to keep the connection alive persists two years later, will leave you intrigued about the twists and turns awaiting in the next chapter of this captivating tale of friendship, nostalgia, and the passage of time."

?

Chapter 5
Roots of Joyful Bonds

As a child, I lived in a small bubble surrounded by the simple love of my amazing parents. Their simple beauty was a treasure mine that changed me at my core. It was in the complex dance of their hopes, dreams, and quiet pride that I learned the power of greatness that doesn't stand out.

Our story starts in the middle of a country area in Kerala, which is like a painting with bright colors of simplicity. The pace of farming and the simple pleasures it brought my Parents shaped life there, like a beautiful melody. Every morning brought a new part in the story of our family, which was written with the ink of hard work, dedication, and the purest love.

When I think about where I really, really come from, my feelings rise like waves hitting the shores of memories. My parents were born there in those horizons of Kerala. The smell of dreams mixed with the sweat of hard work and the laughter of shared moments filled the air in their home. In that safe place, being simple didn't mean lacking something; instead, it meant having an abundance of love, joy, and real relationships.

As they were settled in Jabalpur, both working in different sections of the Indian National Army, in the middle of this country tapestry, my parents built my life from the ground up, like master builders. Even though their dreams were as big as birds, they kept their feet firmly on the ground of humility. It was a tightrope walk between desire and modesty that left a mark on my soul that will never go away. In the embrace of our close-knit community, I saw the magic of sharing problems and having more happiness. Our home wasn't just a building; it was a live, breathing thing that was powered by family ties. Family roots ran through the days, making a fabric that was so strong it could stand up to any storm. Proud that me and my sister were born and brought up in Jabalpur.

Emotions rang through the halls of my childhood like soft whispers. I felt proud inside as I watched my parents handle the tough parts of life with style and strength. When things were tough, the warmth of family wrapped around us like a comfortable blanket and protected us from the world's harsh winds. As the sun went down over those rural areas, I took with me the memories of a childhood filled with simple but deep feelings. The example of how simple my parents were, became the compass that led me through the maze of life. It's a testament to the power of love, humility, and the unbreakable links of family.

Our simple home in the middle of Gun Carriage Factory (GCF), Jabalpur Government Quarters, where everything happened in one single room, was a safe place where we could make and keep happy memories. In spite of how simple it looked, it was like a treasure chest full of laughter, friendship, and the magic of real connection that woven together the threads of our childhood.

As I walk through the halls of nostalgia, I can see our cozy haven, where the walls echoed with the music of our youth. That room wasn't just a room; it was a refuge that protected us from the winds of life and gave us many memories that will last a lifetime. Our small world grew inside those four walls, where we were surrounded by friends, schoolmates and neighbors. The idea of "friendship" wasn't something that happened online or through screens; it was a real, live thing that thrived in the closeness of shared laughter, whispered secrets, and the warmth of human presence. Back when technology wasn't as popular as it is now, our relationships were built through simple face-to-face exchanges that left a mark on our souls that could never be erased by a computer screen. Those were the times of Children playing Hide and Seek, the renowned 'Lattoo", Marbles, Kabaddi, Antakshri, Gilli Danda... Oh My God !! Am not talking about 1857, it was just a few ... few ... some years ago.

The lack of modern tools and conveniences was a blessing that looked like it was making things easier. There were no cell phones that tethered us to screens, TVs that controlled our free time, and bikes or cars that showed off our class. Instead, our wealth lay in the simple joy of shared moments. When we were kids, being simple wasn't a lack; it was a deep richness that gave our days real color.

In this simple world, my Dad became a hero all by himself. With the small luxury of a scooter bike, he got us driven ... err... hauled... ok... ok... ok... ridden to school in Chattra Singh's cycle rickshaw. The simple rhythm of those rides, let us feel Chattra Singh's happiness. He was a local hero who turned our boring commutes into fun times with laughter and friendship. It was more than just a ride; it was a trip where stories were told and friendship stories were whispered by the wind.

As the years go by, these simple scenes come to life and make you feel things. The sound of laughter in that one room, the rides we took with Chattra Singh, and the real connections we made in the safety of our own rooms are the emotional landmarks that show how rich our childhood was. They show that real wealth is not measured by things but by love, laughter, and real connections with other people.

Outside our house, there was a small plot of land that we used for our childhood adventures. It was called the playfield. The place where we grew up was not a fancy stadium, but a simple patch of land. This plain ground held the magic of our laughter, the echoes of our friendship, and the seeds of bonds that would last a lifetime. Playtime spread out like a colorful tapestry of happiness as the sun warmed the open field. There were no strict rules about it like there are in sports. Instead, it moved around in the world of games that made us laugh and strengthened our friendships. We ran through the grass playing hide-and-seek, made boring afternoons exciting with sprint races, and had fun with teamwork and friendly competition in Kite flying and Kho-Kho.

Whenever I think about those carefree afternoons, my feelings spread out like petals. When we played, the grass wasn't just a surface for the ball; it was a holy ground, where dreams came true and friendships were born. Each memory is attached to a different feeling. The thrill of chasing and being chased, spending time in one person's House who got the first Television that I had seen, we all gathered together to watch….. watch Doordarshan actually. The Music and Series part of Door ka Darshan.

Does that happen today in 2024? Can it ??

We had no idea when we were young that Kabaddi, the game that brought us so much joy as kids, would one day grow into something bigger than any of us could imagine. It was only a matter of time before our favorite game spread around the world and made its way to the Olympics. We used to only play simple games in our little world, but now people all over the world enjoy them too. They remind us of the carefree days we used to have. There are feelings and memories of a bygone era mixed together on our simple playfield. To this day, the friendships that were formed through those simple games are a reminder of how powerful play is and how much it changes the course of our lives. We now see that plain piece of land as more than just a playground. It was the stage of our dreams, the ground where our friendships grew, and the place where the memories we hold dearest will always grow.

Sheeba, Noreen, Nisha, Asha, Archana, Rita, Ruba, Gracey, Somi …. Ok.. okkk …Robert, Neeraj, Shantanu… hmmm, I will stop there. The tapestry was absolutely jingoistic. Fun, serious issues like, why didn't she tell us where she was going!

Saturday and Sunday were the days of the week when our homes were jam-packed with fun and happiness. During these special times, Carrom Board and Chess turned out to be the best parts of our weekend trips. There was a symphony of friendship in those golden days, made up of the sound of laughs, the soft clink of coins, and the strategic dance of chess pieces.

The Carrom Board takes center stage as I unwrap the memories that are hidden in the folds of time. I remember how the board, with its smooth surface and worn edges, turned our living room into a battleground where people flicked and planned their shots. As we played chess, our friends and family crowded around and kept their eyes on the wooden board. The striker, a tiny powerhouse, became an extension of our hopes and dreams. Every time we were able to pocket a coin, it sent coins flying and made waves of joy.

I purchased a Carrom Board online three months ago. It stands alone in my room, listening to the sounds of the past. Instead of the usual noise, there is only the sound of the striker hitting the coins. Even though it's a one-on-one game now, every flick makes the room ring with the laughs and friendship of the past. The memories on the Carrom Board are more than just scratches on the surface. They are marks of shared happiness, wins, and the unspoken language of bonds that grow through playing.

Chess sits on the other side of the room like a strange puzzle piece, watching time go by in silence. Its beautiful dances are like a lost melody in the background: they are hard to remember. Chess has become a stranger, an uncharted land ready to be explored. This is in contrast to Carrom, which now dances to a solo beat.

In the back of my mind, the chessboard holds the pieces from games I haven't played yet. Moves that are hard to figure out and fights that never happened are like unfinished sentences that hang in the air. The chess pieces, which have been left alone and patient, seem to be telling stories of moves that have never been made, wins that have never been claimed, and losses that have never been felt. Ah ha... moves that WERE never made, then!

As I wander through the landscape of nostalgia, the Carrom Board and Chess become gateways to a time when weekends weren't just breaks from the week, but also places where people could meet and share happiness. Every piece on the board holds a memory, and every time I look at the games that haven't been played, mixed feelings come up. They tell me that the friendships I made as a child were more than just moves on a board; they are chapters in the book of lasting friendships.

Over time, friends became the quiet constants in the different parts of our lives. Even though we only met them by chance or to wish each other a happy birthday once in a while, their voices echoed in the background of our memories like familiar tunes. Even so, there was a hole in their heart that longed for the warmth of shared laughs and the comfort of faces that were etched in their hearts.

Then, like a soft breeze after a long time of silence, a message came with the hope of getting back together. A dear friend from the past, Sheeba Nisha Mitra (now), who now lives in the exciting city of Dubai, voiced a deep desire to reconnect after 44 years. The words danced on the screen, bringing not only a message but also the chance to light up the friendships that seemed to have died out over time.

Feelings shook inside like bugs waking up after a long sleep. The thought of a reunion made me feel a wide range of emotions, including joy, nostalgia, and a deep longing. The gap, which seemed huge and impossible to fill at first, was now filled with memories of happy times shared in the past. Plans came together in the internet world. Messages were buzzing with excitement, and every keystroke was filled with the desire to make new experiences and remember old ones. The thought of seeing each other again after decades apart brought up feelings that went beyond the virtual space. There were hugs that had been put off, laughs that had been silenced, and stories that had been left unfinished.

As the day of the meeting got closer, our hearts were filled with a wide range of feelings. It gave me hope to think about seeing an old friend after 44 years. It shows how strong friendships can be even when time passes. Just thinking about seeing Sheeba's face, who had been a familiar part of our childhood, made me feel a flood of feelings, including happiness, gratitude, and a strong sense of connection that went beyond the years of being apart.

The day finally came. Together laughing and getting back in touch with old friends filled the hole that had been there for forty-plus years. The reunion was more than just a get-together; it was a celebration of strength and the ties that time and distance could not break. During those special moments, feelings were free to flow, like a river finding its way after a long, winding journey. It was a reminder that real friendships, even ones that are far away, can turn time into a beautiful tapestry of shared memories.

The long-awaited day finally came, and it had an air thick with memories. We got together at the Indian Coffee House in Sadar, Jabalpur, even though we all had our own families by this time. The sight in front of us was overwhelming—people we knew from when we were kids who were now grown up and had stories written on their hearts. The air was electric with excitement, and as we looked at each other, it was clear that this meeting would bring back a lot of memories.

The Indian Coffee House, which stood still and watched the time go by, was the setting for this emotional meeting. As we walked into its familiar arms, the walls seemed to reverberate with the sounds of laughing and secrets we had shared as kids. Not only were we getting together with old friends, but we were also reuniting with pieces of our past. It was a chance to open memories that had been gently shut by time. Hugs that were warm and true helped people who had been apart for years to get back together. Each hug carried the weight of shared history and the hope of new connections. Feelings that had been dormant for years came rushing back to us like a tide. It wasn't just a get-together; it was like coming home. We heard our younger selves in the laughter that filled the Coffee House.

We sipped coffee and told stories while sitting together. The air was filled with the magic of rebirth. It wasn't just a get-together; it was a celebration of the strong ties that distance and time could not break. In the midst of the familiar faces that were now marked with the lines of life, we found comfort in the past that linked us all. The Indian Coffee House, which used to be just a place to hang out, was now a place where old friends got back together. This showed that some ties, even if they are only temporarily put on hold, can bring people back together and make a single day feel like a long-lasting hug.

Can you, think of some of those times in your own Life??

Emotions rushed through the halls of time like a tide, a mix of happy tears and laughter. At that very moment, there was a deep sense of connection and past that they both knew. Personal calls filled with warmth and memories sailed through the air and reached all parts of our lives. People visited homes, which were more than just places to stay. They were places where memories were kept and the sounds of bonds that had been there through all of life's changes.

As soon as we realized we were back together, it was like the choice was written in the stars: this reunion was not going to be short. It was a promise that everyone would do their part to keep the friendships alive and make sure that the embers of our shared past kept glowing, lighting up the paths of our intertwined lives. Unrestrained and real tears of joy traced the lines of smiles that had grown older over time. The laughing, like a melodic symphony, went beyond the years and filled the gaps that distance had created. It was clear that each tear carried a lifetime of feelings, a testament to the strength of bonds that had stood the test of time and distance.

The emotional and committed threads of our reunion wove together like tapestries, making a fabric that showed how strong real relationships are over time. It was more than just a choice; it was a statement that the bonds that held us together would never break, no matter what life brought us. While we looked forward to future reunions, the happiness and laughter of the present became the building blocks of lasting friendship. This made sure that the flame we lit that day would continue to light the way on our shared journey.

Two things that hold our friendship together are constant contact and helping each other out. People don't just talk to each other; they share a symphony of events that connect them on a personal and professional level. This relationship has grown stronger over time thanks to love and care. It's like a fabric that can stand up to the tough times in life.

It turns out that the link they made when they were only a few years apart is more than just a phase. The fact that the friendships are still strong after all this time shows how powerful friendships can be. While we were young, the roots we planted there grew strong and spread across the years, joining us in a web of memories and deep feelings.

It's not just memories that hold us together; these connections are real, living threads that run through our lives. From late-night talks across time zones to words of comfort during hard times, and from shared successes at work to late-night conversations, each event is a knot in the fabric that surrounds us with the warmth of friendship.

Even though our paths have changed and taken us on different trips, the roots we planted in the rich soil of our shared past have not been shaken. These ties are more than just connections; they are the very core of who we are and a warning that, no matter how things change, the core of who we are stays connected to the bonds of the past.

The spirit of family has been a lighthouse for me in the darkest parts of my journey. I found a safe place where acceptance and love could grow in the arms of people I cared about. This place protected me from the storms of life. Some of the things that give me a sense of belonging and purpose are the laughs shared around the family table, the comforting presence during hard times, and the unspoken bond that runs through generations. Each page of this beloved book shows the magic of carefree days and endless fantasy. That's how simple childhood is. I find a source of eternal happiness in the sound of children laughing. It comes from the innocence of those early years. Playground adventures, sharing secrets, and seeing the world with wide-open eyes shaped who I am today. This is 2024 now. Do I see these emotions still? Doubtful! Do you? Do let me know.

There is, however, a quiet force that helps people get through the bad times that life inevitably brings: friendships. The threads that make up a well-lived life are the emotional moments of shared victories, the silent support during hard times, and the comfort that comes from being with true friends. Over time, these relationships become the supports that hold us up when the ground seems unstable. I've learned that living a great life isn't about being the only one standing on top of your own accomplishments. It's about dancing in the joy of everyone else's victories. It's about finding strength in the web of ties that run through our lives. Sharing memories, laughing, and crying together creates an emotional patchwork that is the work of art that gives life its bright colors and deep meaning.

As I take a moment to appreciate the beauty of these connections, a deep truth comes to light: living a great life isn't just about personal successes; it's about caring for the heartstrings that make up a truly enriching lived experience. I'm reminded of an important lesson as I get lost in the emotional tapestry of these connections: live your life to the fullest, but don't forget how important it is to nurture the ties that make it truly rich. Don't let the last part come out until you've fully experienced the warmth of friendships that last.

As a powerful mantra, "Live great as you live" tells us to take every chance for happiness, growth, and personal success. But along with this call to greatness comes the emotional need to not forget to care for your relationships. It's a gentle reminder to enjoy the laughter you share with others, to value the company that makes life easier, and to enjoy the warmth of bonds that last longer than time itself.

The emotional terrain of these connections is a live proof, of how much better life is when enjoyed with real friendship. It's not just a list of things we've done; it's also a collection of feelings we all share that paint a deep picture of our lives. When we look into the eyes of people who have been there for us through the ups and downs of life, we see the real joy of living a great life.

So, as the sun goes down each day, let's remember to water the mental gardens of the people we care about. When we reach the end of our lives and look back, let the memories of laughter, the joy of shared moments, and the strength that comes from strong friendships be the jewels that shine on the path we've taken. Don't let the curtain go down on your life until you've experienced the emotional depth that real connections bring. This is what makes a life not only great but deeply important.

For me, " God gives us great Friends" ... here, the Government gave us Great Neighbors!

"In the corridors of St. Aloysius, where school memories echo, my journey took an unexpected turn when I failed a math test. The shockwaves of a second division in the 10th standard results shattered my parents' dreams of me becoming a doctor or engineer. A crucial conversation with my father unfolded, leading to a pivotal decision—I chose Commerce over conventional options. This unconventional choice became my compass, guiding me to success in the 12th board exams. Amidst the dance of alphabets and financial equations, the chapter closed with the revelation that life's surprises often emerge from unexpected failures and courageous choices. As the curtain falls, the reader is probably left wondering about the twists and turns that await in the next chapter."

?

Chapter 6
Growing up to be a leader and Picking My Own Path

When I think back on my school years at St. Aloysius, memories that have stood the test of time come flooding back to me. That bittersweet day when I said goodbye to the holy rooms that held my formative years may have been 34 years ago, but the memories are still as vivid and alive as they were then. In the middle of Jabalpur, St. Aloysius was a haven of knowledge that held more than just books and classes. It was the center of my upbringing, shaping not only my academic path but also the foundation for a complete and meaningful life.

Image a young heart, full of both joy and fear, entering the world of St. Aloysius for the first time. The air was thick with the smell of excitement, and the unknown was looming big. With each passing day, though, that uncertainty turned into a familiarity that was comfortable, like a warm hug from an old friend. My school years were like a tapestry, with teachers, books, and laughter in the halls creating the threads.

During those years, emotionally charged times like precious gems were spread out widely. These feelings—the thrill of doing well on a test, the friendships formed through shared hardships, and the pride of representing the school in competitions—made up the emotional fabric of my time at St. Aloysius. Every success felt like a win for everyone at school, not just me. It was a cause for celebration that brought us all together.

In reality, though, life is like a fabric; it has both light and dark parts. Leaving St. Aloysius was a bittersweet day. Feelings were strong when friendships formed in the rough terrain of adolescence had to face the natural test of being apart. Once heard in the hallways, laughter now carried a sad note, a song of goodbyes. The walls that saw us grow were still and took in the tears and promises that were offered.

Despite the passing of time, those emotional currents did not go away; instead, they turned into a source of motivation. Lessons learned, bonds treasured, and St. Aloysius's indelible mark on my life became like guiding stars. Feelings from those years are not just memories for me; they are live, breathing things that continue to shape my view and fill my journey with warmth and gratitude.

The choice my parents made about our schooling is like a heartfelt melody in the tapestry of my childhood. Growing up in the loving arms of hardworking government workers, my sister and I were at a point where we could neither afford nor reach our goals. Kendriya Vidyalaya was the best option because it was the main school for many people in the same situation. But my parents had a bigger plan than just making money, so they picked a different path for us—one that would leave lasting emotions on the canvas of our formative years.

Just like now in 2024, getting a prized admission in St. Aloysius was difficult. Fortunately, for me at least, across the Boundary wall of Aloysius. Next door, St. Joseph's Convent H. S. School was a Co-ed School. I think at least for starter lower classes. The same great reputation both the schools had. Without hesitation, my Parents decided to get me admission there – largely a girls School, but here was my lifetime opportunity. Grabbed it. Just like today. Later on, my sister, younger than me, too got admission in St. Joseph's. These were just not a choice; it was a statement that goals were more important than convenience. The journey started with a simple registration form and turned into a deep commitment to giving us an education that was more than just affordable. It wasn't just schools that St. Joseph's and St. Aloysius were for us; they were the places where our growth and hopes were acted out.

Mrs. Jude Pinto is the unsung superstore of this part of my Life. Teacher in St. Joseph's, Mother of 2 of my closest friends, pretty young ladies, so now Aunty Jude for me, surprisingly a regular connect, even on Facebook, and someone, who I was meeting after many Months, walked across to me in Church and asked me to give her a motherly hug. Aunty Jude, you are so loved! Mrs. Jude Pinto was also my Lead Speaker at the inauguration of the Jabalpur Consultancy Division - : "I Know Myself".

Do we know ourselves? Do the Young adults, who are growing up, seeking careers, know themselves? They need to ... to access and use their Strengths and identify areas of further Development. That is what my training is all about. Pure personal experience, translated to communicating with the people who need it.

However, after completing my First Standard, St. Joseph's was stopping Co-Education and would be privy to only the ladies to study there. The next step for us was to hop across the wall and try and succeed in getting admission to St. Aloysius Boys H. S. School.

Ironically, today when I go to Aloysius, It's a co-ed School !!! Admittedly, I am Jealous !!

I still clearly remember the first day, when I stood at the gates of St. Aloysius feeling both excited and scared. The big, scary building seemed to be telling secret stories, and the air was filled with the excitement of something amazing. Every step in those holy rooms made the choice to not go with the cheaper option feel more real. The adjustments they made and the late-night talks they had to make sure our dreams came true showed how much they cared.

During parent-teacher meetings, where the seeds of our potential were talked about and grown, our feelings got stronger. The joy in my parents' eyes as they heard about our accomplishments showed how much they had given up. They had emotional problems as well as financial ones. This showed how strongly they believed that education was more than just a trade; it was an investment in our future.

The choice to go to St. Joseph's and St. Aloysius became a moving story of growth as the years went by. Graduations were more than just events; they were emotional turning points that marked the end of shared goals and the start of new ones. The trip showed how important it is to make decisions based on feelings, and the value of education went beyond the numbers.

When I think about it now, the choice my parents made wasn't just about schools; it was about creating a musical score of feelings that would last our whole lives. St. Joseph's and St. Aloysius were more than just places to learn; they were also places where our ideas took flight and our journeys were given meaning. They gave us not only an education, but also a legacy of emotions that still affects our lives.

Think of the halls of St. Joseph's, where I walked with a sense of discovery and excitement. Being one of the few boys at a school for girls made me feel like a figure in a story about someone who is different. The initial awkwardness turned into laughs, and I found a friendship that went beyond normal rules. The shared secrets, the group projects, and the unsaid understanding that went beyond gender were all emotional parts of those days. As time went on, St. Joseph's became more than just a school. It was a place where memories of old friends could be kept.

There were many feelings on the first day at St. Aloysius. A little fear came from seeing new people and being in new places, but it quickly went away when they felt the warmth of the group. The classrooms were full of the promise of learning, and every contact I had strengthened the picture of how my education was changing over time. Moving to a new school was more than just a change of habit; it was a way to grow as a person and in school.

At St. Aloysius, new friendships were made and the old ones that were made in the holy halls of St. Joseph's were retained. Being strong was the mental thread that linked the two parts of my school life. The emotional lessons that my trip taught me were how to adapt, accept change, and feel like I belonged in different places.

When I think back to my early days at St. Joseph's and then the move to St. Aloysius, I understand that the feelings I had at the time are like the colors on a canvas of my memories. Each school had a different vibe that added to the rich tapestry of my growing years. At the time, the choice to switch schools was scary, but it became a thread that tied together the story of my education, which was full of laughter, friendships, and the emotional turning points that make up a life's journey.

It was in the heart of St. Aloysius that I had a moment that changed the way I relate to numbers for years to come. It was my fourth standard class unit test in math, and it was the event that sealed my fate. The field of battle? In a mid-term unit test, there were four questions, two on Least Common Multiple (LCM) and two on Highest Common Factor (HCF). This makes it a very tough test for Binu Varghese in fourth class. I had no idea that this test would become a compass that would lead me from that early fight to the 10th standard and through the complicated world of numbers. I got each of these 4 questions wrong and got a big zero... a ZERO that I have never forgotten.

That fourth grade test made me feel like I was on an emotional roller ride. I became frustrated and confused as I tried to understand ideas that seemed to be just out of reach. It felt like navigating through a maze of uncertainty every time I tried to solve the questions because the numbers on the paper were becoming elusive enemies. Even though it was hard, there was a spark of determination—a refusal to give up on what seemed like an intellectual Everest.

With the passing of the years, the mental landscape of my mathematical journey changed. Backward steps in the beginning were not problems, but ways to get better. Every mistake I made taught me something, and each lesson made me stronger. At that point in time, it wasn't just about getting over the fear of numbers; it was also about getting over the fear of failing.

From simple math to more complicated ideas in math, the climb became a spiritual ascent. When you reached the emotional peak in the 10th grade, it wasn't just about being good at math; it was also about being good at sticking with things. When they reached that important goal, they felt a deep sense of accomplishment, a mix of relief and joy. It was like coming home emotionally, and I realized that the problem I had in fourth grade hadn't defined my mathematical trip; it had just set the stage for a successful one.

When I think back, I can see that the feelings that were involved in those early battles are what make me strong in math. The fourth standard test used to be a scary opponent, but now it stands for growth and persistence. It taught me that feelings, like anger or drive, are an important part of learning. From having trouble with math to feeling like they had mastered it, their journey showed how emotional strength can be found in every academic challenge, turning problems into victories.

In the hallways of St. Aloysius, I saw a student who was having trouble transforming into a front-bench powerhouse and a natural leader. Evolution happened like a story, with feelings running through every scene. Starting as being appointed as a class monitor in the 5th and 7th grades and working up to the prestigious role of Red House Vice-Captain in the 11th grade, the seeds of leadership were planted, indicating a period of personal growth to come.

A leader's first few days were a mix of uncertainty and excitement. The job of being a class monitor made me feel obligated, which made me doubt my abilities. Despite this, the weight of the post sparked a change. Friendships with peers, shared successes, and even occasional setbacks were emotional turning points that shaped how I thought about leadership.

For me, as the years went by, the mental landscape of my leadership journey changed. Getting elected to the position of Red House Vice-Captain in the 11th grade felt like a big accomplishment. It showed that my classmates and teachers had faith in me. Beyond the title, that accomplishment had a deep emotional impact. It made me feel like I had taken on a duty to inspire and guide others.

Nevertheless, being elected as the "School Captain" in my last year was the highlight of my school career and something that I will always remember. That moment was emotional to the point of being overwhelmed. Beyond a title, it was an honor to be recognized for growth, toughness, and the heartfelt leadership of both mind and heart. There was a symphony of feelings that echoed through the school halls: my parents' pride, laughter from peers, and applause from teachers.

In hindsight, those early leadership roles were like planting seeds in St. Aloysius's rich ground. Not knowing at the time, these small roles were laying the groundwork for a career outside of school. Those moments of leadership, whether it was the initial nervousness or the later sense of success, shaped my future career in public speaking, leadership training, and eventually business consulting.

Being a tentative class monitor to being the School Captain wasn't just a change in Designations; it was also a story of emotional growth and self-discovery that happened in the quiet hallways of St. Aloysius. I became a leader by using the feelings I experienced as a student who was having a hard time to find his voice and purpose. St. Aloysius wasn't just a school; it was a place where leadership was formed and where my feelings became the guiding stars of my personal and professional growth.

When I was wanting more in school, I rediscovered a love that would change the very core of who I am: Basketball. It was something the basics of which I learned and played in my Primary School days, living in GCF. The small group which played there, incredibly had girls playing along with us. Toolika Naidu ... hmmm... one single name that I still remember. Toolika was that one single girl, who came to play with us boys and then a few others followed her. Toolika and me continue to be great Friends. Common interests and things to do in Society and Friends groups, hold us together. We often comment about 32 years ago! Meeting almost every year in these last few years is a rediscovery of a mutual depth of attachment and togetherness. Indian Coffee House !! For me, the Basketball court was a safe place where every dribble and shot made me feel better. The excitement of the game temporarily took the place of the difficulties of the textbooks, and it was during those times that I discovered a part of myself that the textbooks could never show me.

The trip into the world of basketball was a big change for me emotionally. When I made my first basket, it felt like more than just a physical win. It was a victory over self-doubt and a boost of newfound confidence. As a team, the highs and lows of success and loss became emotional threads that woven a tapestry of strength and passion.

Amidst the sounds of basketballs bouncing, a new chapter began: debate. I had no idea that the power of words would add another stroke to the picture of who I am. Standing on the national stage and winning a gold award in debate, was an emotional high point that seemed out of this world. There was a symphony of feelings that echoed long after the debates were over. The rush of putting ideas into words, the adrenaline of the competition, and the shared wins with my debating team. It was there I learned the power of expression in words and deeds. Speaking out. Speaking out in front of relevant gatherings.

Debates are not 'arguments.' They are putting across your views and beliefs and questioning the rationale behind views that oppose the matter of the moment. Read that line again.

Hobbies like basketball and debate weren't just things I did for fun; they were how I shaped my character. Feelings I had on the court and at the debate stage seeped into my being and shaped who I am in ways that books could never do.

A transformation took place in the maze of obstacles and victories. I went from being a student trying to figure out how to get through school to being more—a positive motivational speaker and a useful Trainer for leadership and people development. The emotional elements of this change were like notes in a melody; they all worked together to make my new identity sound good.

When I spoke in front of a group as a motivational speaker for the first time, I could feel the nervousness and joy. Sharing personal stories made me vulnerable, and I wanted to inspire people. Together, they made an emotional tapestry that linked me deeply with the audience. Not only was there a change in real space when I went from the basketball court and the debate stage to the podium, but I also learned more about myself and grew emotionally.

When I think back on this trip, I can see that despite the difficulties, I found passions that became important parts of who I am. Basketball and debate weren't just hobbies for me; they were emotional landscapes where I learned things about myself that I could never learn in a textbook. The love of the game, the thrill of the argument, and the growth into a motivational speaker and trainer were not just parts of my life story; they were emotional turning points that made me who I am today.

However, I was still a tentative student from 4th class onwards till the TENTH grade, where the dreaded Board exams stared at me.

In the 10th grade, when the dreaded Board test results came out, it was a turning point in my life. The highs and lows of excitement crashed into a hard reality: they just barely made it with a second division. That piece of paper was heavy not only because it had my grades on it, but also because it held broken hopes, both mine and my parents'. In those days, becoming a doctor or engineer was seen as a normal path to follow. But suddenly, the second division result, leaving behind a scary feeling of uncertainty.

At an emotional level, telling my parents the news was like walking through a trap. There was a storm inside me because I was waiting to see how they would respond, afraid of disappointing them, and open to the consequences of how well I did in school. The moment of discovery turned into a cliff, where the dreams of a planned future and the harsh realities of life met. I had passed my High School, but a Second Division result glared at me... hmm... glared at my parents' views.

As I stood in front of my parents, the room was heavy with dreams and hopes that had been dashed. Their hopes, which had been carefully put together over the years, were now in danger. There was worry, and maybe even a little sadness on their faces, which showed how society put a lot of pressure on people to be successful in a narrow sense. It was a turning point where my academic problems were seen not only as a personal problem but also as a departure from the normal path in society.

After that realization, I reached a turning point in my life. Now, the need for reevaluation was more important than the hopes of following a traditional job path. It was a time for me to think about myself and find a new way forward by drawing on my skills and passions. Letting go of societal expectations and accepting a different story caused a lot of emotional turmoil. It was both freeing and scary.

Even though there was a lot of doubt, a seed of strength was planted. The emotional upheaval of that time made them even more determined to show that success and worth could be measured by a person's own standards, not just by their test scores. The next step was also a path of making a deliberate choice for the future of my life.

From now on, I can see that the moment in 10th grade wasn't just about test scores; it was about breaking free from society's rules. I had to rethink what success meant to me because of the emotional waves of sadness and self-doubt. It wasn't just a change in how well they did in school; it was also a change in how they thought and felt, which set the stage for a more real journey ahead.

My academic path came to a halt when my dad asked me what I wanted to study in the 11th grade. There were only two choices: science or arts. In that same year, though, the divine opened a new door. Commerce as a subject was introduced. This unexpected offer was a moment of huge joy for me.

My talk with my dad went like a careful dance of words, with feelings bubbling under the surface. I felt hesitant as I thought about the few options that the school world offered. Because science is so prestigious, my dad thought about bargaining with the school to get me into it. His thoughts were on going into uncharted territory, and his silent worry about my future cast a shadow over the room. But in that tense situation, I said "no" to the idea of going into science. That moment carried a lot of emotional weight; it was a statement of who I am and what I want to achieve.

Choosing to go into Commerce was more than just a choice; it was a turning point that showed how important it is to go your own way.

Emotionally, it was a rough road from that discussion to choosing commerce. Commerce's uncharted area made people both excited and scared. The emotional complexity was raised by the weight of societal standards that came from the traditional respect for science. Making the choice wasn't just about meeting deadlines; it was a statement of independence and a departure from the beaten road to a place I chose.

The emotional terrain of my choice became clearer as the 11th standard went on. Business and numbers weren't the only things that commerce was about for me; it was also about finding a way to combine my skills with a passion I had. The friendships I made with other commerce students, the fun of learning about business ideas, and the feeling of control over my academic path were all emotional benefits that were much greater than the initial worries.

As I look back, the decision I made to go into Management studies even though it went against what most people thought was the right thing to do became a moving part of my life. A story about finding out more about yourself, being strong, and having the mental courage to go against the 'rules.' The talk with my dad wasn't just about what to talk about; it was also about our hopes and dreams, and how to find the right mix between what society expects of us and what makes us happy. The path from that firm "no" to a fulfilling academic goal shows how embracing one's own path, even when uncertain and emotionally turbulent, can change things.

When I think about that important choice, I'm filled with a lot of different feelings. It's like a fabric made of threads of self-discovery and strength. It's a choice that now shapes the lessons I teach as a Life coach and team leader. That moment at the crossroads is more than just a part of my life; it's a guide star that shapes the values I hold dear.

The way that moment made me feel is like a soft hum in the background of my entire career. It's a warning that a parent's hopes and dreams for their child, which are often based on the prestige of jobs like doctor or engineer, shouldn't drown out the child's own hopes and dreams.

Supporting self-awareness is more than just a job for me; it's a promise that comes from the emotional echoes of my journey. I learned how important it is to know your skills and weaknesses in the hallways of St. Aloysius, where options seemed limited. Having to fight my feelings when I had to stand up for my own dreams despite what other people thought made me want to fight for independence.

As a professional career guide today, it's touching to see how students feel as they try to make sense of all the options. They have the same kind of sparkle in their eyes when they understand their unique strengths, the same kind of vulnerability when they talk about their fears, and the same quiet determination, to make their own paths. It's not just about making choices about school; it's also about emotional awakenings and the search for identity in a world where success is often predetermined.

When I lead a team, the emotional threads of choices I've made in the past affect how I care for my team. Emotional investments based on personal experience include knowing the unique strengths and weaknesses of each member, making a space where each person's goals are respected, and encouraging a culture of self-awareness.

The lessons I now teach aren't just theoretical; they're infused with the mental strength I've gained from making the choices I have. As a career guide and a Trainer, you don't just have to make sure that students follow their passions, help them find the right job path, and stress how important it is to know yourself. They are the emotional links between making choices about school and going on a deep journey of self-discovery.

As I think back on this trip, I realize that the emotional echoes of that important choice are not just memories; they are living principles that give me advice in life. The promise to put a student's dreams ahead of societal expectations and the understanding that everyone's path may not always fit with the norms are more than just lessons learned; they are emotional legacies that continue to shape my story as a career guide and team leader.

This change from struggling with the mysterious world of mathematics, which was full of formulas full of letters that seemed like an unsolvable puzzle, to accepting the world of business was more than just an academic one. My school life changed directions because of a transformation, a journey with mental highs and lows.

My former enemy, math, and I had an emotional dance that made me feel beaten at times. Mathematical puzzles and numbers seemed like an impenetrable wall. These feelings—frustration at not understanding the ideas, self-doubt, and fear of failing—made for a storm of emotions. It was a personal battleground where every attempt to understand felt like a small win and every mistake like a disastrous loss.

The decision to move into Commerce, which included 'Management' as a subject to specialize in, felt like emotionally entering uncharted ground. Feeling relieved that the algebra nightmares were over was mixed with both joy and fear about what was to come. With the possibility of a new academic environment, commerce became a lighthouse of hope and a door to a new chapter that could change how I felt about school.

When the 12th board exam results were released, this journey's emotional peak was met. Not only did seeing my name on the State Merit list confirm that I had done well in school, but it also represented a victory over the challenges I faced in math and a testament to the strength I developed through hardship. The fights and victories led to strong feelings of pride, relief, and success.

My life story unfolded on the canvas of St. Aloysius's victories and tragedies. Beyond academic successes, the emotional turning points of the journey were the building blocks of a real, meaningful life. People's friendships with peers, teachers' help, and personal struggles all added emotional depth to the canvas.

Thinking about this part of my life, I understand that switching from math to Commerce wasn't just about fitting subjects into a schedule; it was about finding joy in learning again, discovering my strengths, and choosing a path that fit in with my interests. This decision still affects the choices I make today, telling me that school isn't just about grades; it's also about the emotional landscapes that shape our identities and pave the way for a life full of authenticity and purpose.

During the most important years of my life, deep lessons taught me that real success is more than just getting good grades or fitting in with what society expects of you. This story is about a person's emotional journey as they follow their interests, face challenges with unwavering determination, and find the courage to make their own unique path. With its indelible mark on the canvas of my mind, St. Aloysius is still my guiding light as I walk through life's ever-changing landscape.

In the classrooms and hallways of St. Aloysius, I came to the idea that success isn't limited by grades. The emotional realization happened during both happy and sad times. The emotional fabric of my academic journey was made up of the friendships I made with classmates, the support I got from teachers, and the struggles I had with myself.

I learned that real success is like a tapestry that is made with love in the arms of St. Aloysius. Igniting the flame of one's own hobbies is just as important as meeting the expectations of others. Finding my interests while I was still in school was like finding a compass: it had a strong emotional impact and showed me the way forward.

The challenges I faced along the way turned into mental turning points, and each one made me stronger, which is what makes me who I am today. When I doubted myself, was afraid of failing, or had to fight an uphill battle, those were mental valleys. But with each step, I came out stronger. It was a path of finding out more about myself and building up my emotional strength. Facing challenges became a rite of passage, turning problems into stepping stones.

When I think about those formative years, the feelings of making my own way still come back to me. I had a lot of feelings when I decided to go against social traditions – some of them which I found outdated- and write my own success story. It meant letting go of the need for approval from others and being willing to be vulnerable when following one's true passions.

St. Aloysius is still my compass because of the caring setting it provided and the emotional marks it made on my soul. The emotional connection that was made inside those walls is still a source of power and motivation. The lessons I learned in those holy halls help me find my way through the complicated dance of life. They're like a compass that points to being true to yourself, being strong, and following your interests as the true signs of success.

The main idea behind my story about my time at St. Aloysius is that our mental journey shapes how we think about success. It's more than just a chapter in the book of life; it's a story about accepting feelings, facing obstacles with courage, and finding meaning in following your own path. St. Aloysius is more than just a school; it's a safe place where feelings and learning come together. It has had a lasting effect on who I am today.

"In the vibrant corridors of St. Aloysius, the school experience transcended the ordinary, with School Principal Dr. Fr. Davis George at the helm. Known to all, Fr. Davis left an enduring impact as both a strict disciplinarian and a source of inspiration. As students moved beyond the school gates into the global corporate arena, his teachings became a guiding force. Amidst tales of fantastic teachers and extraordinary experiences, a cryptic phrase, emerges, teasing readers with an unknown secret. This enigma sets the stage for a narrative filled with surprises and twists, inviting readers to uncover the mysteries that lie ahead in the unfolding chapters."

Chapter 7
The Guiding Light of St. Aloysius

Let me take you back to the good old days of St. Aloysius, when every moment was a precious gem in our memories. At the center of it all was the amazing Dr. Fr. Davis George, who was our school's crown prize.

When you think about this amazing person, you must be feeling a warm smile spread across your face. Fr. Davis wasn't just a Principal; he was also a living inspiration, a guiding light, a strict but loving teacher, and most of all, a dear friend. Even though years have passed, the memories of school still come back to me, and Dr. Fr. Davis is still a bright spot in my life, even now in 2024. His effect didn't stay in his office; it spread to every part of the school, a good force forming our personalities and plans for the future.

Oh, the stories about how strict he was are written in the books of our past. But it wasn't a harsh enforcement of rules; instead, it was a concert of discipline and values that will stay with us long after we leave the comfortable embrace of the school gates.

Picture this: it's a cool morning, and the sun is just starting to shine softly on the courtyard. As Fr. Davis walked in, we students would gather for the School Assembly, looking forward to seeing him. The regular School Anthem, The Prayers to St. Aloysius, the Schools Patron Saint, the National Anthem, and the announcements would be routine. Yet, what we waited for was for Fr Davis to walk up and speak to the students. Wasn't daily, wasn't the usual, but each expression was a profound flow of words and emphasis on what needed to be done and what was expected from Aloysians. His presence would make us respect him. Unspokenly, everyone knew that he wasn't just there to keep things in order; he was also there to teach and guide young minds.

His presence and eloquence, weren't just lessons from a textbook; they were life lessons wrapped in stories that showed how to be strong, kind, and push yourself to do your best. He wasn't making us into obedient followers; he was making us into future leaders by teaching us how to be kind and have the guts to do what's right.

And when the hallways were full of laughter, it was usually his quick wit that set the mood. It wasn't just a distant echo; his laughter was a melody that brought us all together, making ties that went beyond the student-teacher relationship. There were times when things were hard, but Fr. Davis didn't just hand out punishments; he also reached out to understand, which said a lot about how much he believed in our ability to learn and grow.

Even now, years later, when life throws me curveballs, Fr. Davis's lessons become a compass that guides me through the storms with the unwavering strength of the values he taught in those holy halls.

St. Aloysius wasn't just a school; it was a place where people were shaped, and Fr. Davis George was its heart. There would have been many wonderful Principals before his term, but for us, he was an inspiration, a guardian of ideals, and a friend whose influence lasts forever.

While Fr. Davis may have seemed far away to some, he was a calming presence for students who were having a hard time with their schoolwork. Each student's problems touched his heart, especially those who needed extra help. His care for us went beyond books and grades; he truly wanted the best for us. He saw promise where others saw problems, and for those who fell, he was more than just a principal. He was there to help us, brush off the fears that were sticking to our uniforms, and gently push us to take another step forward.

I still feel painful memories of taking difficult tests. In those situations, Fr. Davis's ability to understand shone the best. The hallways could feel like a maze of stress and worry when everyone was studying for tests, but Fr. Davis had a special way of picking up the mood. For St. Aloysius students, his words were like a lifesaver, a secret code that could break up the hardest times into pieces that were easier to handle.

He would keep saying and it lifted our spirits when we were feeling down. Our shoulders suddenly felt a little lighter, and the maze of test stress seemed easier to get through. A mantra, a reminder that echoed through the hallways, it wasn't just a bunch of letters; it was a way to know that we weren't alone on this hard trip.

I still clearly remember those times when the walls of the classroom could see how nervous we all were. Instead of giving harsh lessons or acting coldly, Fr. Davis didn't react. He instead became a warm light that radiated understanding and compassion. Every syllable he spoke had a deep meaning: every stumble was a stepping stone, and every struggle was a chance to grow. Fr. Davis wasn't just our Principal- the Head of the School., but a person giving us advice at that time; he was a rock of strength standing next to us as we anticipated the unknowns of exams. The sincerity in his voice made us feel better; it reminded us that he understood our problems and treated our journey with respect.

I remember those school days because of both the academic skills I learned and the way Fr. Davis taught me to be strong emotionally. In addition to shaping our brains, he also changed our hearts, leaving an indelible mark on the tapestry of our lives.

Teachers at St. Aloysius were more than just teachers; they were skilled 'craftsmen' who wove a web of information and direction. As we went through the maze of education, they were always there with us, their unwavering dedication shedding light on the sometimes, confusing road.

Each teacher added a different color to our learning. They weren't limited to the stiff pages of textbooks; instead, they brought themes to life through stories, examples, and sometimes a bit of humor. It was like they had a magic key that opened the doors to understanding with each interesting lesson. Oh, it wasn't just what they said that made it magical; it was how much they believed in us. When we were having doubts about ourselves and the path ahead seemed cloudy with confusion, our teachers were like lights of unwavering faith. Their support didn't just last for a moment; it was a steady flow of believing that reached deep into our being.

This was not a business deal where information was exchanged for grades. It wasn't just a friendship; it was a deep relationship that went beyond the classroom. Our teachers didn't just see us as students; they saw us as people with hopes, fears, and dreams. They took the time to read not only what we wrote in our notebooks but also what was written in our hearts.

So, as we think back on the mosaic of our school years, let's not forget the colors that these amazing teachers added. They planned our progress, watched over our potential, and turned the classroom into a safe place where we could learn and share experiences. It's not just that the teachers at St. Aloysius were teachers; they were also the builders of our academic journey, and their influence is still felt today.

Let me paint you a picture of the wonderful people at St. Aloysius who did more than just study for tests and read books. They made learning and growth sound like a beautiful symphony.

There was Sir Tiwari, who was great at math and turned hard tasks into fun ones. His excitement about numbers wasn't just a lesson; it spread like wildfire through the classroom, accepting even those who used to be afraid of math. Imagine how happy you would have been if complicated math played out like a thrilling game, turning your fear into interest. Remember Binu and his Mathematics? The 4th standard LCM and HCF?

Then there was Mr. Gregory, who could go back in time. He didn't just list times; he told stories that turned dry lists of dates into interesting journeys. We had more fun in his classes than just learning. There were Mrs. Callaghan, Sir Sharma and the 'caning stick' Branded Sir Daga. They were like going on a journey through the halls of time. All of a sudden, subjects weren't just a list of facts; it was a story that made us wonder about the stories that our world held.

At St. Aloysius, it wasn't just about school; it believed in caring for all of its students' needs. As I remember the now 'out-of-fashion', Kneeling down under the school Bell, you please picture the school on the Annual sports day- as a sea of cheers from students who became the biggest cheerleaders and rallied behind each other on the field. What more could you want from a competition? It was a celebration of teamwork, energy, and the happiness that comes from winning together. The stunning show of Gymnastics had young Aloysians flipping through the Fire Rings, The sprints and the relays – passing the Baton from one to the other, as they sprinted out to win.

That is a life lesson that I carried throughout my Career and even today. Sprinting, passing the Baton, and crossing the winning line first. That is a line that 'certain' persons, today, need to read again… and again !!!!

Oh, and the School's Annual Show every year! The stage turned into a dream world where even the shyest students found secret skills. It wasn't just a show; it was a journey of self-discovery. It was a time when confidence took the lead and shyness faded. People were cheering for more than just the actors. They were cheering for courage and the magic that happens when people step onto the stage.

Each teacher and event in St. Aloysius' life was like a thread in a tapestry that told a story of growth and joyous discovery. They were more than just teachers; they created an environment where learning wasn't a chore but a fun journey of self-discovery and shared successes. Emotions danced, dreams flew, and the essence of education went beyond the usual in those holy halls, leaving behind memories that lingered like the sweetest melodies.

Thinking back on those school years, I see that St. Aloysius wasn't just a place to learn; it was a place where I learned important things about life. Not only did we have to memorize facts or do well on tests, but we also had to find our inner strength, make friends that would last, and learn how important it was to have teachers who believed in our abilities.

But when things got tough, Fr. Davis would say a mantra or a secret code: "Tertiary Success" Once practicing for a Debate competition, he made me repeat the word- "Tertiary Success" 30 times to get the pronunciation right. These words were more than just a bunch of letters; they were a strong warning that problems are not obstacles, but steps that lead to success. The words of that chant are still playing in my head, like a beacon of hope that says, "You can do it."

Thanks to St. Aloysius, school wasn't just a part of a book; it was a story that shaped us into the people we are today. It's a celebration of the times we learned how to do more than just survive. A heartfelt Thank You to Fr. Davis and all of our amazing teachers who, like skilled navigators, made sure that our educational journey was not only safe but also life-changing, leaving marks that will never fade in our memories.

Dear Fr. Davis. Your student here, ultimately did get 'tertiary success' right in life.

"The story took unexpected turns as the leaves of my childhood at Aloysius School unfolded. School life extended beyond academics, involving me in social events such as Nehru Bal Sangh's National Integration Camps, which foster cultural exchange across India. Following graduation, I founded Navchetana, a youth organization that outperformed expectations by holding functions on par with metropolitan standards. The Catholic Church Youth Group adds a spiritual component by highlighting the everlasting wisdom of the Ten Commandments. The path led to major responsibilities in the national youth movement, culminating in a momentous moment, selected as a Keynote Speaker at the World Youth Day gathering with, Pope John Paul II as the Guest of honor. Another one was three days with Mother Teresa left an unforgettable imprint, leaving me wondering whether she was rewarded, or the Nobel Prize was. Transitioning to professional life, the ominous phrase "Sarcoidosis" cast shadows on the tranquil environment the School had bloomed into a magnificent tapestry."

?

Chapter 8
Understanding Life Outside of the Classroom

The magical world of school life, where the smell of texts mixed with the excitement of tests, was home to a lively world beyond the school day. It was a world where social events and the friendships of student groups were important, and it opened up my world beyond the classroom. My path into the Nehru Bal Singh Organization was one of these beautiful parts.

Imagine a canvas filled with the colors of variety, where students from all over India came together for the Annual National Integration Camps. These camps weren't just get-togethers; they were rainbow-colored parties of understanding and unity. The makeshift tents we stayed in during the trip were the most exciting part. There were little Indians in every corner. My feelings were running high when I saw seven to eight kids, each one from a different state, staying in the same tent. For 10 days, together. In those canvas walls, it seemed like the very soul of our country was captured. Lots of people were looking forward to it, interested, and eager to learn more about each other's cultures.

Nagaland and Calcutta lived together in the comfort of our tent, and Kashmir and Bihar told stories to each other. Goa brought its own taste to the mix of cultures. As we talked about traditions, customs, and funny things that happened in our hometowns, the tent turned into a mixing pot of feelings. It was moving when a student from Kashmir talked about how beautiful his snow-covered home country was. His eyes sparkled with pride, but there was also a desire for the familiar chill in the air that was there. Missing home and the thrill of representing a different culture danced together in a sweet way.

Around the center of this mix, bonds grew like wildflowers in a meadow. We laughed together, made mistakes in each other's languages, and became close even though we lived in different places. The togetherness we felt wasn't just an idea; it was a real thing that was woven into the fabric of what we had in common. The 10 days included activities like State Cultural Group Dances, Debates, Groups singing, Fervor of Patriotism ran through us- Kashmir meeting Jabalpur, Calcutta saying Hello to Cochin, Bombay cutting across to Calcutta. The Food that was served, the Guests who came in, I was amazed at the plethora of the mix of India as a Nation. Integration of the Nation is what that was, is what it is, is what it should be!

As the sun went down and turned the sky orange and pink, our different groups stood together, showing how beautiful it is to be united in differences. We weren't just students from different states at that point, under the vastness of the night sky. We were a group, woven together by understanding, kindness, and the joy of being a part of something bigger than ourselves.

Because of the laughs, tears, and cultural exchanges that happened inside those canvas walls, Nehru Bal Singh became more than just a group of people. It was a safe place for me to express my feelings and a special part of my school life. There are hundreds of us still bonded together, in various cities, the bonding and binding of a mission forms common platforms, decades later. It was just three days ago that Archana Somashekhar, came home with Preeti Chowdhary. We were meeting after 38 years! Spending some wonderful time together, we did find a common platform to tread on. Together. Each of us were into People Development, separately. People are meant to cross paths again in life when they are meant to. People are there. Persons are there. It is the connection that is missing. Sort of missing... yet, the call for bonding and being together is there. Looking forward to an exciting and useful journey with the soulmates that I am Blessed with.

Once I got past the school gates, I came to a turn in the road. Since Nehru Bal Singh was an Organization for school Students, it doesn't work for me now that I'm not in school. When I saw this problem, it made me more determined than ever.

I made a personal effort and created something new. Friends joined hands and presented to Jabalpur was 'Navchetana.' A new awakening.

In the small town of Jabalpur, where I was the Founder President of Navchetana, my idea came to life. It wasn't just a group; it grew into a thriving society with a limit of 100 members. What surprised and encouraged me was that almost half of these people were strong young women who were becoming leaders in their own right. It wasn't just a meeting; Navchetana turned into a brand that beats, a sign of unity and shared goals. Feelings ran high as the group grew, and each person was a symbol of the teamwork we encouraged. Among the heartwarming stories, the rise of involved girls as leaders was a shining example of how to give people power. Their trip was like the Navchetana philosophy: they broke stereotypes, accepted differences, and helped each other.

This small town called Jabalpur saw Navchetana grow into a well-known force. Our events were not just blips on the radar of the community; they were a part of its life. As a culmination of our work, the Annual Function went above and beyond what was expected. A live fashion show began that was as bright and stunning as those in busy cities like Bombay and Delhi. Probably, the First ever Fashion Show organized in Jabalpur, in a public forum.

During these wonderful moments of chaos, I wasn't just tied to school-related things. Being a part of the Catholic Church Youth Group opened a new stage in my life. There wasn't your usual church talk about morality or catechism. Personal growth could happen there, new ideas could grow, and spiritual lessons helped us find our way through life's maze.

In the middle of the chaos of the world, the Ten Commandments, which are written in the Holy Bible, stood out as guiding lights for a happy and balanced life. Accepting these timeless principles wasn't just a ritual; it was an emotional trip that made us think about ourselves and led us in the right direction.

My feelings get stronger as I think about this life-changing trip, from the tents of Nehru Bal Singh to the colorful fabric of Navchetana and the spiritual haven of the Catholic Church Youth Group. This is a story about more than just events and groups. It's also about strength, resilience, and how shared dreams can change a person's soul.

A timeless verse stuck with me in the Bible: "Ask and you shall receive; knock and it shall be opened to you; seek and you shall find it." The words are simple and not very complicated like Shakespeare's, but they say a lot. It wasn't just a verse; these words became a lighthouse that showed us how important it is to act in our lives. We can't expect others to understand our wants if we don't go out and actively seek opportunities. In the Training Programs that I conduct today, I often mention, Ask, Seek, Knock.

Do we actually ask? Do we actually Seek? Do we actually Knock? If we don't knock, how will the doors open? If we don't ask, how will it be given to us? If we don't seek, where are we heading to? AS youngsters growing up? As People Seeking Careers? As ambitious as we may be, where is the direction to fly to?

This phrase became the beat of my work as my journey in the youth movement went on. From a small beginning, I worked my way up to become the State President of Madhya Pradesh. The effects of my work could be heard across the area and all the way to the national level. When I reached these important goals, I felt happy, but I also knew that each step was a representation of the words I kept close.

That's when something happened that will always be a part of my life. Think about being on a world stage and speaking for your whole country. The stadium was packed with thousands of people at the World Youth Gathering in Denver, Colorado, USA. Pope John Paul II stood tall on the podium of that big stage. With confidence in my body, I gave a 15-minute speech that spoke to the hopes and goals of Indian youth.

But what happened afterward was even better than the attention. When I bowed my head to the Pope, he did something I didn't expect. He got up, pulled me close, asked what my name was, and then gave me a warm hug. In that moment, captured in a picture that is still treasured, the lines between normal and extraordinary became less clear. The Pope's action went beyond rank and implied a sense of shared humanity that didn't need words.

At that very moment, I felt a rush of thanks, humility, and a strong sense of connection. Not only was it a chance to take a picture, but it was also a deep recognition of the path, the battles, and the strength that got me to that point. The quote that once made me do what I did echoed louder, reassuring me that when we ask honestly, the world will sometimes give us unexpected, warm hugs in return.

I had the amazing chance to spend three days with Mother Teresa, which marked the beginning of a very important part of my life. I was with a small group of young people when I was a part of an experience that went beyond religious and political lines. At the elderly care center of the Missionaries of Charity, we went from one bed to the next together, with Mother Teresa's presence lighting the room like a soft ray of hope. She spoke to all of the elderly residents with the same kindness, even if they were from different faiths or countries. This simple act, this real connection, echoed the language of kindness, which is understood by the heart and not limited by labels. For Mother Teresa, this was a regular activity. For us, it was a once-in-a-life moment.

One thing from those days stuck in my mind very clearly, and it showed me how humble Mother Teresa was. Even though, that particular day, one of the rooms smelled foul from the trash, she didn't act rude or uninterested. She chose to clean up the mess instead, so she grabbed a broom, a bucket of water, and a cloth. It was a powerful example of how she thought real service went beyond words and into deeds.

At that very moment, the air was filled with the quiet strength of humility. Being a role model for kindness and charity, Mother Teresa didn't shy away from the less glamorous parts of care. She did more than just preach; she lived by the principles she believed in. Seeing her stoop down to pick up the trash left a lasting mark on my soul. It taught me a lesson in humility that I still feel today.

Mother Teresa was kind, but she was more than that. When she talked to the person in charge of keeping the room clean, another side of her personality came out. In that stern moment, she showed a different side of herself, a warning that compassion could be both soft and firm when other people's safety was at risk.

People still talk about those three days, and the sound of them reminds them of the lessons they learned with a holy person. Even though the room was clean of physical mess, what was left was a deep understanding that true and unwavering compassion sometimes needs a strong attitude. With her broom and bucket, Mother Teresa not only cleaned a room, but she also swept through my heart. She left behind a tradition of kindness, humility, and the belief that kindness has no limits.

When I completed College, I left the carefree days of youth and went to work, where the rhythm of life was set by the routine of a monthly paycheck. The need for financial security became a painful truth that changed the color of my life.

As I moved through my career, health was still uncharted ground, untouched by the walls of hospitals. But, as I went along, there was one word that kept coming back to me—Sarcoidosis—and it has become clearer over the last two years. There it was, a whisper of doubt, an unwelcome guest that made the unfolding stories of my life more complicated.

Over the course of my time at Aloysius School, the seeds I planted began to grow into leaves, casting shadows and shaping my path beyond the familiar walls of education. The skills I learned in school were now being used in real life, and they were like beacons leading me through the ups and downs of adulthood. In the business of work, a symphony of events played out, with each note teaching a useful lesson about how life works. Unity's harmony echoed a tune that reminded us how important it is to stick together when things get tough. Compassion, which was a part of who I was, came apart in times when sensitivity became the link between hearts.

One important lesson stood out: it's important to take the lead. It was at Aloysius School that the seeds of proactive involvement were planted, and now they are blooming in the form of confident steps taken in the professional world. The courage to take the lead, to start change, and to step forward became not only a lesson for me but also a driving principle for my life.

But as life went on, Sarcoidosis cast a dark cloud over the colorful picture. It was always there, a silent reminder that health problems could happen at any time, even when you were working hard on your job or growing as a person.

Despite these feelings, the trip went on. It was a delicate dance between what was known and what was unknown, between what was familiar and what had not been explored. The experience leaves rustled, telling stories of strength, growth, and how deeply all of life's threads are linked. As I went forward, the memories of Aloysius School followed me, now mixed with the unknowns of health. They were like a compass helping me find my way through the uncharted areas of adulthood.

?

Chapter 9
Inspiring Spirituality and bowing to the Divine.

Dear Reader, if till now this seems to be a journey of everything being perfect and straight, allow me to bring in something different. Great friends and close Friends, many times have scars that develop. They develop as we bloom, grow, and sort of think that we understand everything within Planet Earth.

This is not radically different; many have watched this taking place. However, most have remained silent, quiet. Observers we are, sidelines we prefer, and nothing wrong about it. However, I always felt the need to express myself. To speak out. Not arrogantly, not abusive, good boy Binu has been. Yet, remaining silent observers is equivalent to acquiescence – agreeing- as we didn't speak up opposing if we did feel it was inappropriate.

This was largely the period of 2022 and 2023. It was about a 'Battle' between Religion and Nationalism.

One of the National Debates that I participated in was in Delhi. I was representing Madhya Pradesh.

The topic was "Religion is the greatest separatist force in India"

Binu Varghese spoke FOR the motion.

Binu Varghese won the Gold Medal.

That was many years ago. I notice now that I could have been an Astrologer, predicting things to come years later. Today.

Without getting into the details of what I expressed, then, allow me to put my perspective into context.

THERE IS ONLY ONE GOD AND HE HAS NO RELIGION.

My 1989 High School WhatsApp Batch of 114 classmates, grown up into Daddies now, are split into three groups. 3 and a half termed as Radicals, 2 and a half termed as "Pseudo Seculars" and 107 silent spectators.

Not that we meet often. But now I tend to believe that WhatsApp is a curse. Specified purposes.

Again, will try to keep this simple- as it's not related to my friend Sarco.

My Close Friend, very personally close since as a kid, Sangeet Verma put it in perspective, as he sat with me and spoke.

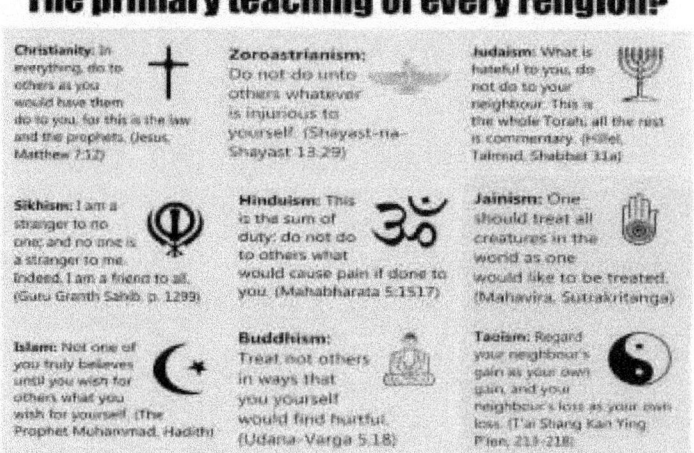

I know I am hopping from Headline to Headline.

There is no competition between the Holy Books of any Religion and the Constitution of my Country.

Period.

Full Stop.

People who have participated in a Nehru Bal Sangh National Integration camp will understand the strength in me. I cannot have my

Patriotism to my Nation questioned. Or even linked to the Religion that I follow. Few are people who have stepped into Churches, Temples and Gurudwaras. Not for sight-seeing, but actually kneeling and praying to the Almighty. Binu Varghese does so.

For the Three and a Half Radicals, my Friends:

Am an Aloysian, just like you are. However, am Special.

As an Indian Citizen,

Nobody in the World can hate you like I can.

As an Aloysian Friend,

Nobody in the World will love you like I can.

Read those two lines once again.

A song (in Hindi) that I love and get inspired by. I chose it for the School Assembly conducted by me, on the 150th Year of St Aloysius Schools establishment.

इतनी शक्ति हमें देना। दाता, मन का विश्वास कमज़ोर हो ना,
हम चलें नेक रास्ते पे हमसे, भूलकर भी कोई भूल हो ना...
हर तरफ़ ज़ुल्म है बेबसी है - सहमा-सहमा-सा हर आदमी है,
पाप का बोझ बढ़ता ही जाये - जाने कैसे ये धरती थमी है,
बोझ ममता का तू ये उठा ले - तेरी रचना क ये अन्त हो ना...
दूर अज्ञान के हो अन्धेरे - तू हमें ज्ञान की रौशनी दे,
हर बुराई से बच के रहें हम, जितनी भी दे, भली ज़िन्दगी दे,
बैर हो ना किसी का किसी से, भावना मन में बदले की हो ना...
हम न सोचें हमें क्या मिला है, हम ये सोचें किया क्या है अर्पण,
फूल खुशियों के बाटें सभी को सब का जीवन ही बन जाये मधुबन,
अपनी करुणा को जब तू बहा दे कर दे पावन हर इक मन का कोना...
हम अन्धेरे में हैं रौशनी दे, खो ना दे खुद को ही दुश्मनी से,
हम सज़ा पाये अपने किये की, मौत भी हो तो सह ले खुशी से,
कल जो गुज़रा है फिर से ना गुज़रे, आने वाला वो कल ऐसा हो ना...
हम चलें नेक रास्ते पे हमसे, भूल कर भी कोई भूल हो ना...
इतनी शक्ति हमें दे ना दाता, मन का विश्वास कमज़ोर हो ना...

"There was a regular ad in the newspaper (I guess that Naukri.com didn't exist then), that made me apply for a job as a Junior Sales Officer. That was the first big step in my journey with Nestle India. When I got to Bangalore, I was excited to take on the task of selling well-known brands like Maggi Noodles and Milkmaid. But, my goals went beyond sales goals. They pushed me to come up with new ideas and do more for the business and my career. I got four promotions in ten years, which led me to Nestle India's Head Office. As a senior manager, I had to deal with a lot of different tasks, and I was always looking for the next challenge to help shape Nestle's future and my own job. I'm still looking forward to the next part, which I know will have more surprises and victories in my Nestle odyssey."

Chapter 10
Stepping into Success

Once upon a time, I was just like any other dreamer going through the tunnels of life. Consider this: I was flipping through the pages of a newspaper when my gaze was drawn to an advertisement from Nestle India Pvt. Ltd. The words blurred into a sea of possibilities, and there it was—a magnificent opportunity for a Junior Sales Officer, a chance waiting to be taken.

The mere thought sent shivers down my spine. Without hesitation, I spilled my dreams into paper and hit 'send.' Hope floated in the air, a delicate promise of what could be. Days passed, each one accompanied by an anxious heartbeat, until the word I had been waiting for finally arrived—I had been shortlisted for a personal Interview. My heart raced with joy and expectation, and I couldn't believe my good fortune.

The day of the group discussion and personal interview approached, and I could feel butterflies in my stomach. It seemed like I was on the verge of a new chapter, the pages of which held the mysteries of my destiny. Jabalpur, my backdrop, was suddenly whispering my name in enthusiastic murmurs. The Aloysian Training and experience in verbalizing, asking questions, Leadership, putting in suggestions- The Personal Interview and the group Discussion was a 'Hit the Nail on the Head'. News of my foray into the world of Nestle, the FMCG behemoth, spread like wildfire among my friends and family.

Imagine the emotional rollercoaster—the pride in my parents' eyes, the joy in my friends' voices, and the slight nod of acceptance from my mentors. It was more than simply a job; it was the affirmation of my dreams, a stepping stone towards a future I had dared to conceive. I was on the verge of a voyage, the road ahead packed with possibilities. Emotions cascaded like a waterfall when I accepted the post of Junior Sales Officer. The first sale was a triumph. The difficult days were a test of endurance. Throughout it all, the camaraderie with coworkers became the fiber of my professional story. The emotional tapestry weaved with the strands of hard effort, commitment, and the occasional setback became the story of my development.

As I marked a year in this dynamic adventure with Nestle, I think about the emotions that have colored the pages of my story. Every emotion has carved itself into the story of my work, from the excitement of acceptance to the trials that shaped me. As the sun sets on another day, I look forward to what the next chapter brings, equipped with the lessons of the past and the emotions that continue to fuel my path.

It seems like only yesterday when I arrived in Bangalore, loaded with drive and dreams of making it big as a Junior Sales Officer. Nestle's excellent portfolio of products—Maggi Noodles, Cerelac, Lactogen, Milkmaid, and Chocolates—were my traveling companions. Little did I know that this adventure would become a pivotal chapter in my life, complete with ups and downs and a slew of emotions.

The first few days were a mix of exhilaration and trepidation, similar to stepping onto a stage for the first time. Each shop I visited carried the promise of fresh opportunities, and with each order placed, a wave of accomplishment warmed my heart. Maggi Noodles, a well-known household name, became more than just a product I sold; it became a connection to people's homes, their shared memories over a quick dinner. It wasn't just about selling; it was about making memories and forming friendships and associations, now with the retailers.

In the midst of the hulla-boo, I came across moments that marked my path. There were days when a little store owner's grin after a large order boosted my determination. Each rejection became a stepping stone rather than an obstacle. These were emotional milestones, reminders that success is often a combination of modest successes woven together with tenacity and enthusiasm.

The years passed, and my dedication was not unappreciated. My story at Nestle unfolded like the pages of a novel. Four promotions in ten years, each one a monument to the blood, sweat, and tears poured in this rollercoaster ride. The familiar surroundings of shop visits were turned into the corporate ambiance of the Head Office. I was promoted to Senior Manager, with responsibilities that extended far beyond those initial shop-to-shop conversations. The bustling streets of Bangalore became my daily canvas, and the shopkeepers became the characters in my story. Convincing people to embrace Nestle's products was a delicate ballet of connection-building. Every interaction became an opportunity to learn about their environment, listen to their wants, and empathize with their problems. Walking into those stores was like walking into the life of the people behind the counters. It wasn't simply about selling Maggi Noodles or Milkmaid; it was about becoming an answer to their everyday problems. As the sun blazed down on the streets, I learnt to accept rejection as an opportunity to improve my approach rather than a setback. It was a path of resilience, recognizing that behind every refusal was a narrative of a business owner struggling to make ends meet or confronting obstacles beyond my comprehension.

Emotional moments bloomed like buried pearls in the middle of the city's bustle. There were times when a shopkeeper's reluctant smile morphed into a nod of agreement, signaling not just a sale but the beginning of a collaboration. These were the occasions that ignited my desire, the emotional currency that propelled my trip.

The adventure was about more than just wandering the streets; it was about navigating the complexities of human interactions. It was about turning the act of selling into a symphony of comprehension and problem-solving. As the days evolved into weeks, and the weeks into months, the relationships I formed became the foundations of my success. Each shopkeeper was more than just a customer; they were a part of a shared journey, and Nestle's products were more than simply objects on shelves; they were solutions to problems faced by people working for a better tomorrow.

The journey, like any worthy experience, had its share of ups and downs. Some days, the sun beat down relentlessly, making the pavement too hot to walk on, and my feet cried for relief. Yet, in those difficult times, I discovered stepping stones, each one encouraging me to rise above and prove my mettle. Selling wasn't simply a career; it was an expedition of self-discovery—an opportunity to find my hidden skills and push beyond the constraints I once felt constrained me.

There were days when the obstacles appeared overwhelming, like climbing a mountain with no end in sight. The constant heat reflected the pressure I was under, but instead of allowing it to scorch my spirit, I used it as fuel to propel me ahead. Each rejection was not a closed door, but an open window through which I saw the tenacity within me, a resilience that transformed setbacks into opportunities for future success.

Looking back, the journey was a symphony of emotions—joy, disappointment, determination, and pride. From a wide-eyed Junior Sales Officer to a seasoned Senior Manager, each step vibrates with the heartbeat of an amazing epic, a story written with the ink of dedication and engraved with the colors of Nestle's success. Those years held a unique place in my heart, and it wasn't just about selling items; it was about weaving a tapestry of passion and commitment. Each day, I set out on the road with a simple yet deep question in mind: "What more can I do for the company and my career?" It was about pushing limits, exploring unexplored territory, and discovering innovative methods to make a significant contribution.

The journey from Junior Sales Officer to Senior Management became a narrative of progress for me. Promotions were more than just title changes; they were acknowledgments of the battles fought and successes won. The Head Office, which was once a distant fantasy, became a physical symbol—a tribute to what perseverance and hard work might accomplish.

Among the promotions and advancements, there were emotional moments that created the picture of my trip. There were days when the exhaustion was unbearable, but a customer's thanks for recommending the appropriate Nestle product served as a soothing balm. The camaraderie with fellow salespeople became coworkers warmed the corporate ascent. It wasn't just about climbing the ladder; it was also about cherishing the friendships formed along the way. That extended to various postings in different places, Technical Training in Nestle's Largest Manufacturing unit in India, Moga in Punjab, Sales & Development projects in Calcutta, Bombay, Cochin and back to the Head Office in Gurgaon.

The Head Office, with its frenetic energy and high-stakes judgments, became more than just bricks and mortar. It became a representation of my ambitions, a reminder that each step forward was a testament to the perseverance that fueled my journey. The sweat-soaked days and sore feet were not simply physical consequences, but badges of honor, worn proudly as a reminder of the resilience that defined my story.

Looking back, the trip wasn't just a series of promotions; it was a symphony of emotions—a composition of tenacity, resilience, and the steadfast belief that with each difficulty met, a greater version of myself developed. The searing sun and tired feet were not hindrances, but rather companions in the magnificent adventure of self-discovery and success.

Reflecting on the past, I see a younger version of myself, someone who dared to take a chance, submitted that job application, and joyfully embraced every opportunity that presented itself. The road wasn't always easy, but the bumps were like threads woven into the fabric of a worthwhile voyage. Nestle, once just a workplace, has evolved into a dynamic stage for personal development and latent success.

In this remembrance of my journey with you, I find myself imploring you, my friend, to be fearless in taking risks, to welcome difficulties with open arms, and to fight the allure of settling for the usual. Life is a journey, and each step is an opportunity to learn something new about yourself. It's not always about ease; sometimes the actual diamonds are found in the battles, in the moments when you rise above adversity.

There were emotional moments that defined my voyage. I recall the tense exhilaration of applying for the job and the fear of the unknown. The first day at Nestle was a mix of uncertainty and possibility. Each obstacle presented itself as an opportunity to demonstrate persistence and tenacity.

Nestle turned into a canvas where my abilities were painted and goals gained flight for me. The bonding with colleagues, shared achievements, and even the collaborative overcoming of hurdles were emotional monuments on this path. Times when the burden felt overwhelming, but the support of a team transformed colleagues into companions on this voyage.

As I offer my hand to you, my friend, in honor of starting my career, I encourage you to live fully. Embrace the unknown, relish the challenges, and don't settle for the mundane. Life is a fascinating tapestry of events, and each day is an opportunity to color it with your own distinct hues. So, don't just exist; live passionately, and who knows what extraordinary destinations your voyage will reveal!

?

"After an enriching 11 years with Nestle, our protagonist seamlessly transitioned to a new chapter with Associated British Foods plc. Ltd, UK, Mauri division—the global leader in fermented yeast and bakery ingredients. Starting as the Business Manager for South & West Asia, including India, I swiftly relocated to Bangalore. In a mere four years, a meteoric rise ensued, catapulting them to the position of Managing Director overseeing all countries in South and West Asia. Reporting directly to the London-based CEO, the protagonist found themselves at the helm of a global empire, embarking on a thrilling globe-trotting adventure. The reader is left captivated, wondering about the twists and turns that will unfold in the dynamic world of international business and corporate strategy."

Chapter 11
Being open to growth and change

As the pages of "DON'T DIE BEFORE YOU DIE!" turn, they show an emotional story full of changes, personal growth, and trips around the world. The main character is about to go through a big change. They are an experienced person who has worked at Nestle for 11 years. Our hero leaves the familiar halls of Nestle and enters the unknown world of Associated British Foods plc. Ltd., Mauri business.

When our main character takes this huge step into the unknown, you can feel all of their feelings. It's not just a change of companies; it's a deep transformation—a change of duties that is full of hope and excitement. Feeling a little nervous and excited at the same time about taking on bigger responsibilities on the world stage.

As the goodbyes ring out through Nestle's halls, feelings are like a whirlwind. Coworkers who have become friends say their goodbyes with tears in their eyes, and the air is heavy with pride and memories. In the midst of this emotional storm, the main character leaves behind a legacy of shared laughter, difficulties met, and bonds formed in the fires of corporate life.

The scene changes to the beginning of a new story, which takes place in the busy city of Bangalore. The next step in our main character's journey is painted on this city, which is full of the lively energy of the business world. The chance to become the Business Manager for South & West Asia, which includes India, is a big step toward growth and a change in where you live.

Among the busy streets and cosmopolitan noise in Bangalore, our main character finds a new beat. There are a lot of different feelings in the city, from being afraid of change at first to being excited about exploring new business territory to a soft longing for home that pulls at the heartstrings.

This Chapter "DON'T DIE BEFORE YOU DIE!" is more than just a job change. It's an emotional symphony, with each note playing the melody of growth, courage, and the unwavering spirit to face life's unknowns.

In the middle of the Mauri division's world, I as a Senior Business Manager, dives right into the interesting world of fermented yeast and baking ingredients. As the global leader in this specialized field, the Mauri division is a formidable figure. It weaves a tapestry of challenges and opportunities into the main character's story. There are mixed feelings of excitement and anticipation as I get to know the details of the new work environment. It's not just the smell of yeast and baking ingredients that becomes important; it's also a sign of the mix of difficulties and successes that are to come. It's a journey that transcends mere job tasks; it's a voyage into a world where passion for one's work becomes the driving force.

As you turn the pages of the professional narrative, you'll see that hard work and commitment are the unsung heroes. The main character draws a picture of dedication and hard work over Years. The office becomes like a second home, and the noise of the machines becomes a familiar tune that plays in the background of their work life.

My journey then takes an exciting turn, like the ending of a well-written story. A raise is like a beacon on the horizon of your career. Feelings are crazy—a heady mix of pride, success, and maybe even a little doubt. The well-earned rise to the position of Managing Director is both a personal victory and a testament to the hard work and determination that got them there.

The main character is now at the wheel and is in charge of steering the ship for the many countries in South and West Asia. This duty makes me feel both humble and strong. Once more, the emotions change, going from the thrill of the climb to the sobering understanding that being a leader has its own set of problems.

Having to report straight to the CEO in London makes the emotional journey even more complicated. There is a link between people in different places, a bridge made of trust and knowledge. No longer is the main character's story just about reaching job milestones; it's also a tale of personal growth, resilience, and the emotional echoes that can be heard in the halls of professional success. In the middle of business plans and boardroom choices, my journey is powered by the human emotion that drives each step forward.

Yet.. yet.... yet... what is not forgotten even in this distant place and a long time back are learnings of Teamwork, Friendships, Empathy, Team Work and building success stories TOGETHER !!!

Binu Varghese's meteoric rise is more than just a climb up the professional ladder; it's also a story full of adaptation and resilience. The story builds up like a tapestry, with threads of problems, successes, and the emotional weight of managing a business world that is always changing.

As the Managing Director, I get onto a stage where being a good leader is the most important thing. It's not enough to just make strategic choices; you need to be able to change, come up with new ideas, and dance through the complicated steps of cultural differences. On my journey, there are emotional moments where problems aren't problems but stepping stones and failures are chances to grow. It's about merging and walking along with the people and cultures of Countries like Sri Lanka, Pakistan, China, and Nepal, a dive into the clutch of different Countries in the Middle East and so many more. Hops into Australia and the UK, added to Raising the Bar for my own strengths and learnings from my Childhood days.

In this part of the story, the term "Managing Director" becomes more than just a name. It's a base from which our main character not only leads but also motivates teams in different parts of the world. You can feel the pride in your accomplishments, the weight of your responsibilities, and the soft hum of excitement that comes with the chance to make a good difference in the world.

The start of traveling around the world is a key event in this story. Now as a true global citizen, I set out on a trip that went beyond borders and time zones. Each trip brings a wide range of new experiences, so the mental suitcase is full of hope. From the busy markets of India, where every deal is a heartbeat in the rhythm of business, to the prestigious boardrooms of London, where decisions are heard across countries, each place the main character visits helps them learn more about the global business world.

With each passport stamp, the range of emotions grows. There are exciting times when you meet new people, difficult times when you have to adjust to different work cultures, and moving times when you realize that everyone wants the same things. There are times, like during jet lag and conference calls, that make you feel good, like when people get to know each other over shared meals, when laughter can get past language hurdles, and when teams work together across miles. In this chapter, the Managing Director does more than just lead; they also act as the emotional center for teams as they navigate the complicated world of global business.

This part of my journey is all about how I felt about accepting change. It starts with having the guts to leave the safety of a familiar job and go into the unknown, where people from India have rarely gone before. The story beats with the blood of courage, a strong feeling that propels our main character into a new chapter.

Giving up what you know and moving into the lively embrace of Bangalore is a change that affects more than just your body. Cities with lots of tech-savvy people can be great places to start a journey for both career and personal growth. The feelings are like threads that run through the fabric of change: the nervous excitement of the unknown, the excitement of new tasks, and the subtle thrill of possibilities opening up.

I get to the heart of the story through the job of Managing Director, which is like having a captain at the helm. As responsibilities grow, so do the feelings, and the ship of leadership sails through the fast-moving currents of the food business. The person in charge feels both proud and humble as they steer the ship. They know that being a leader isn't just about making choices; it's also about creating an environment where people work together and come up with new ideas.

In the fast-paced world of food production, where each item has its own story, employees not only lead but also tell stories. The emotional moments are like plot twists in this story. They include the pleasure of overcoming problems, the camaraderie that forms with a team of people who are passionate about their work, and the times of reflection where personal and professional growth meet.

The feelings are like a symphony as the chapter goes on: the melody of courage, the harmony of new ideas, and the beat of growth. Bangalore is more than just a city; it's a character in this emotional journey, showing how I have grown from a beginner to a leader who sees change not as a problem but as a chance to make the story more interesting and satisfying.

In this interesting chapter, the main character's interactions with people from different countries and teams become a source of inspiration. The trip goes from the busy markets of South Asia to the high-class business districts of London, weaving together a rich collage of different experiences. This story is full of emotions like joy, learning about other cultures, and the subtle thrill of connecting with people from all walks of life.

As Managing Director, your job is more than just carrying out business strategies; you are also responsible for building bridges and encouraging people to work together across countries. When people meet for work, their feelings flow through them like a river, bringing understanding, empathy, and a common goal of success. The main character not only becomes a leader but also a cultural ambassador. They have to find the right balance between business goals and the personal relationships that support them.

As the pages turn, the reader sees not only how the main character grows professionally, but also how they grow personally. The emotional events—the sense of accomplishment that comes from overcoming problems, the joy that comes with wins, and the lessons learned from setbacks—are like milestones on this trip. Each event adds a thread to the tapestry of strength and growth.

The chapter brings the idea of "DON'T DIE BEFORE YOU DIE!" to life. It turns into a lighthouse that tells the main character to live fully and welcome every twist and turn. When the main character is weak, this theory comes through emotionally. They find strength not only in successes but also in accepting the lessons that failures bring.

As the story goes on, I found myself on the edge of a huge, linked world, ready to start a journey of discovery, learning, and leadership. It's easy to feel the excitement in the air, and this phase is full of the allure of uncharted lands, unexplored views, and a strong spirit ready to thrive in the face of change. As I start this global adventure, am filled with excitement—can't wait to figure out the mysteries of new places and connect with the cultures that are just waiting to be found.

The emotional moments are like sparkling stars in the night sky; they lead me through unknown territory. There's a mix of excitement and fear, like a tourist who steps foot in a new country, unsure but full of the promise of life-changing experiences. The heart beats with the rhythm of excitement, just like I am ready to face the challenges and take advantage of the chances that lie ahead.

"New Horizons" is more than just a figure of speech; it's a real thing that can help you grow as a person and in your career. A lot of the emotional landscape is made up of times when the main character learns not only about the world but also about how much they can do. Each task turns into a chance for emotional victory, showing how well I can handle the journey's ups and downs.

"Life took an unexpected turn when Sarcoidosis barged in, leading to my grounding and a swift departure from the mundane realms of employment. Amidst the chaos, I clung to sanity, navigating a labyrinth of hospitals and a bewildering array of 21 prescribed medicines. Binu Varghese hovered on the periphery, raising questions about pharmaceutical intrigues. Juxtaposed against the surreal weight gain of a basketball player pumped with steroids. Left on the edge, wondering what unpredictable twists awaited in the enigmatic pages of my life."

?

Chapter 12
Finding Your Way Through the Medication Maze

Life played a game I didn't sign up for, with all of its unpredictable turns and twists. Sarcoidosis jumped into the story and turned my world upside down, making it more complicated. When it happened, it was like a storm—unexpected and strong—and I had to pick up the pieces of my once-orderly life. The routine was gone, and I was faced with the hard truth that I had to quit the job I loved.

During the chaos, my feelings were strong, and I could feel a symphony of fear and doubt in my heart. I could feel the inner turmoil as I tried to come to terms with the sudden end of the life I had known. Every day turned into a battlefield where they had to fight to keep things normal in the face of the unknown.

It was an emotional roller coaster ride as the medical journey went on. It was a crazy trip into the unknown. When hospitals were once strange lands, they became an unwanted second home where I sought safety. Every visit was a search for clues, a last-ditch effort to solve the mystery that my body had turned into. It took a huge toll on their emotions, and their screams could be heard in the clean hallways of hospital facilities.

The medicines I was given, 21 of them in all, became my constant friends. Each pill came with its own set of directions, a guide to help me find my way through the maze of my worsening health. Taking so many drugs was hard on my emotions, and the emotional weight got heavier every day. It was a routine, a never-ending cycle of pills and potions that made me realize how fragile my life was.

In the middle of this medical chaos, times of weakness showed up. The quiet tears that fell as I tried to deal with the harsh truth of my situation. The bittersweet embrace of loved ones, their eyes mirroring a cocktail of empathy and worry. Each emotional event became a stitch in the fabric of my strength, weaving a tapestry of perseverance in the face of hardship. During everything, I held on tight to my mind. The emotional turmoil never stopped, but I was determined to face the problems that were coming. I may have been off balance when life threw me curveballs, but in the chaos, I found emotional power I didn't know I had.

Fourteen steroids had their own consequences. A lifetime of complexity. The bunch of chemicals became like faithful shadows that followed me through the stages of my day as I went through the complicated dance of my medical journey. The routine was strict; it was a never-ending loop that controlled my day, every morning, noon, and night, before and after meals. It seemed like Binu Varghese, the medicines wizard, had cast a spell that linked my fate to the profits of the big drug companies. There was no escaping the irony: a few months back, I had given my skills to a pharmaceutical company in Ahmedabad for a Free lance Consultancy, and during my short three-month stay, I helped them make more money without even realizing it.

As the pills piled up, so did the weight on my back. My body changed in a way that seemed like it was written by fate. I was forced to be the main character in a story I didn't want to be in. Steroids were sold as medicines, but they had a lot of bad effects that were not meant. My body swelled up to the size of a Weightlifter, rather than the Basketball player I used to be and the scale went through the roof, reading 163 kilos. I saw the irony: the medicines that were supposed to help me get better were changing my body in a way that made me feel like a stranger in my own skin.

This change had a huge effect on my emotions. Each pill I took was a sour reminder of how my body was changing. The mirror reflection became a silent observer of the changes that took place, a visual account of the fight going on inside. During the quiet moments before bed, the weight of the steroids went beyond my body and into my feelings. The products made me wonder what kind of cosmic joke was being played on me. To use a figure of speech, it was a nasty pill to swallow.

Even so, a spark of strength appeared among the mental chaos. I was determined to find my way through this uncharted territory with the same drive that had led me to work in the pharmaceutical business. Every emotional setback served as a stepping stone, showing that the human spirit can survive and change, even when things don't go as planned.

During the chaos of my medical journey, I took time to think about the road I had taken. It wasn't just a fight against a health disaster; it turned into a tough test of resilience, a classroom where survival was the lesson. The days were filled with taking medications, going to the hospital, and dealing with the weight of physical changes. These things weighed heavily on both my body and my mind.

In the middle of the storm, a strange calm appeared. Life showed itself in its simplest form when it was stripped of all its complications. The tricky dance with illness showed us the beauty in things that are simple. It was like the universe's strange design was making me think again about the most basic things in life. You could feel how heavy this journey was on your emotions. As the person swallowed each pill in the hopes of getting better, they were carrying both the medicine and the weight of mental strength. The hospitals' clean walls became witnesses to the silent battles going on inside. The hallways were filled with the footsteps of determined soldiers.

Joy, in its simple form, became a light in the darkness at those times. No longer was a day without pain just a day; it was a victory and a break from the crazy routine that had become my standard. Every small victory felt like a huge accomplishment, and every step forward showed me a power I didn't know I had.

The mental landscape of the trip was filled with shades of thanksgiving. Thankful for the help of family and friends, the kindness of the medical staff, and the peaceful times amidst the chaos. These emotional turning points were the strings that held my strength together, making a tapestry that showed I could survive against all odds. Binza, Ravi, Lavu and Shauru stood out with a support that has been everlasting. Shankar

Bhaiyya was another coin that added up. More about him as we go along.

The steroids, which could both fix and cause trouble, were very important to my story, which was about relying on others and facing challenges. These drugs weren't just medicines; they were a lifesaver, but they had a lot of side effects. They were fighting a quiet war against the chaos in my body, and they were also planning changes that required me to adapt all the time. It became a tightrope walk between needing medication and trying to hold on to a sliver of normality in a life that had been completely turned upside down.

This discovery made me feel a lot of different things. Each pill reminded me of how well I was getting along with the pharmaceutical world. The clean, clinical atmosphere of hospitals, which used to be a business setting, now had a personal meaning. Being both a contributor and a consumer in this link made me feel very heavy. Stepped back into my life, my Classmate Dr. Anurag Sahni and his Younger Brother, Dr. Anupam Sahni. 'Anupam', as I called him and "Bhaiya" as he addressed me… Anurag is DON for me and I got used to DON introducing me as "Captain", to whoever, wherever we met!

While on this drug trip, feelings came to the surface like water waves on a pond. During the routine of taking medications, there were times when I felt vulnerable. This was a quiet way of acknowledging the complicated dance between healing and its side effects. At these points, the human side of the story came out, going beyond the medical nature of the story.

Life's uncertain beauty had thrown me into a story I hadn't planned. Through a series of twists and turns, the field I had worked in before became an important part of my personal story. It reminded me that our lives are often written in strange ink and that each part shows us a strength we didn't know we had.

When things get hard, the human spirit shows its amazing strength, and its ability to adapt and draw power from deep within. Going through hard times turned into a deep study of not only how to survive but also how to really live. The way each day went showed how strong the spirit is that lives inside all of us.

In the maze of problems, a strong lesson became clear: the power of perspective. It was about finding happiness in the little things that happen every day and appreciating the quiet times that pop up like gems in the middle of all the noise. This change in how I thought became a lighthouse that helped me get through the worst times. There was a choice to accept life as it is, flaws and all.

When I was strong, my emotions were like threads running through it. Every task and every win was weighed down by a thousand feelings. During the quiet times, there were tears, not just tears of pain but tears of victory over the problems that had been faced. The emotional scenery turned into a painting with shades of bravery, weakness, and a firm resolve to welcome life with open arms.

These last few pages are more than just a recollection of medical fights; it was a moving story of strength and finding light in the darkest places. I learned a deep lesson that went beyond the medical facts in the book: The key to not dying too soon is to learn how to embrace life with all your heart, even when things are uncertain. The trials were not just physical; they were also emotional journeys that changed the mind in a way that can't be erased. While there was a huge storm going on, the story went through times of weakness, strength, and an unshakable spirit that wouldn't die. The feelings that were a part of each medical trial were what kept the story going.

I could feel the mental toll growing as I learned more about my complicated health. Aside from the bodily pain, it was also about figuring out how to get through the complicated maze of fears and doubts. In the quiet spots of my trip, tears became a silent friend. I cried not only when I was sad, but also when I was happy because I had gotten through hard times. These emotional moments were the heart-wrenching breaks in a story that moved forward with a strong heartbeat. The storm that obscured my way was a metaphor for 'uncertainty' that threatened to put out the small flame of hope. But in the middle of the storm, I found a source of power that could stand up to the darkness. Even the smallest steps and breaths taken in defiance of the storm were heavy with mental weight. It wasn't just a fight against sickness; it was a fight for life itself.

When the revelation came, the story hit its peak: the key to not dying too soon was to be able to hold on to every thread of life, even when the future was uncertain. During those intense feelings, the beauty of life became clear. A simple meal turned into a feast of thanks, and the touch of a loved one became a lifesaver when things looked hopeless.

This wasn't the end; it was the beginning - shows how strong the human spirit is and how important it is to welcome life's unknowns with open arms. This showed that even in the worst places, you could find a spark of life and let it grow into a bright light of hope.

? ? ?

"My life became an interesting trip through a maze of treatments, including Allopathic, Ayurvedic, Acupuncture, and Therapy Massages, after a medical prognosis that was long overdue. Even Naadi Shastra had a time when it was understood. Unexpectedly, my friend Anu Elvis from Delhi helped me find meditation. She brought me to the worlds of Reiki and crystal healing. When skepticism turned into interest, the power of positive energy, which can bypass physical hurdles, became clear. Anuradha Iyer added her voice and told me to relish the pleasures of life. I'm standing on the edge of an unwritten story with a group of consistent friends that includes Shobhana, Callisto, Cassandra, Tresi, Annsi, Annie Bablu, Amit, Sangeet and others. What's next in this mix of old traditions and new friendships? As the tapestry of my life continues to unfold, the curtain flutters, implying surprises and discoveries that defy common sense."

Chapter 13
The Power of Positivity

In the complex fabric of my life, I faced an enemy that put the core of who I am to the test. It was a task that made me think of ways to solve it. It was a battle against an invisible enemy that wanted to cut short my time on earth. With their huge supply of drugs and old cures like Ayurveda, the doctors threw everything they had at it. I started getting massages regularly and exploring more alternatives. Came into my life the mysterious Naadi Shastra.

Still, no matter how hard I tried, time seemed to slip away like sand through my fingers. A six-month deadline hung over me like a dark cloud, marking what was meant to be the inevitable end. But fate had a different plan, and here I am, Four years after what was meant to be the end of that story.

Meditation, which was often suggested as a treatment, came with its own problems. In the noise of my disturbed mind, the peace it promised seemed hard to find. It felt like I needed a touch of godliness, an angel to help me get through the storm inside. Anu Elvis, a friend from Delhi, then showed up as a surprise sign of healing, like a lucky turn in the story.

Anu, who practices Reiki and believes in the healing power of crystals, added a new layer to my search for peace. I was skeptical at first, but I couldn't help but be taken into the positive vibe she gave off. Her strong, faraway presence became a lighthouse that helped me find my way through the maze of uncertainty.

The emotional journey mixed with Anu's unusual ways of doing things. The friendship, the laughter, and the understanding that was shared without words formed a link that went beyond the physical and into the spiritual. There was a dance of forces going on, a delicate choreography that happened while I was struggling.

The mental landscape changed as Anu's healing touch moved through my life. Each Reiki session turned into a moving part of this strange story. The story was about strength, friendship, and the mysterious power that comes from two like-minded people getting together.

The journey went on despite all chances, showing how strong the human spirit is and how miracles can happen when we least expect them to.

My whole viewpoint changed when I virtually met Anu. She was always so happy and positive. Finally, I understood that life is like a tapestry, with lines of hope running through it. Focusing on the moment, hoping for the best, and letting go of the weight of the unlikely are all parts of this. During this trip, I learned about the mind's wonderful power—a force that can beat bad things and lead us to better things.

Another bright spot in my life, my good old friend Anuradha Iyer, helped me change how I felt about things. She brought me hope, gave me confidence, and made me feel proud of myself in a way that I hadn't felt before. Through the challenges, I was able to get through them because of the strong waves of her unwavering support that went through my thoughts.

It was my friends who stood by my side through all of life's ups and downs. Callisto, Shobhana, Cassandra, Judie, Sushma, Mini, Shyja and and and and... It's people like Diana Lobo, Shajan, Sanjay Pillai, Cynthia, Nazrul, Joseph, and a lot of others who make life possible and show how beautiful human relationships can be. Even though they had busy lives, they made time to spend with me, connecting with me and giving me support.

With these people by my side through good times and bad, I had something to hold on to when the storm was about to take me away. It was their simple but meaningful actions that made my hard times more bearable. What made me feel better was their laughter, and what gave me strength was their support. As I look at their names, I see threads of love and thanks stitched into the fabric of life. Their busy lives didn't stop them from being great friends. It became valuable things that money can't buy: their time, their understanding, and their undying presence.

My journey has many names, but Maria Shah's is the one that stands out among all the others that have colored my life. Maria was the first one who asked me to write it down. Fr. Davis another time, another situation. Annsi had been scripting a Book for the last three years when she told me about it. Habitually, I gave her 30 days to complete it and nudged her into completing her Book. She did it and together we got it published and released at a high-profile function in Bhopal. The Book is " UNDERSTANDING THE SELF" and it's a great output for Readers to read. Annsi continues the walk and we look forward to some more to come.

After going through a lot of healing, Maria became a lighthouse and an example of how positivity can change things. It's not just a silly catchphrase to make you feel good; it's a powerful game-changer. I learned that positivity is the magic that can change the impossible into the doable. It makes a holy space in our lives where the extraordinary can happen.

During this trip, the mind is like a captain guiding a ship through the rough seas of negativity. Maria's impact kept me from going into dangerous waters like a gentle wind filling the sails. When she was around, I felt like the ship of my life was setting sail for the lands of hope. Maria's constant happiness mixed with my problems made me feel strong emotions. It turned into a way of life, not just a theory. In my thoughts, her words of support echoed through the halls, a melody of strength that blended with the noise of my doubts. The way Maria thought about the power of a positive attitude and her thought that I was meant to assist other people helped me find my way out of the dark places of depression.

Through the ups and downs of problems, Maria's name became linked to strength. I found a friend, an ally, and a guide in her. They were more than just acquaintances; they had a link that was made of understanding and shared victories over hardships. I look at Maria's name as a thread of motivation in the big tapestry of my life. It shows how one person can have a huge impact on another person's journey towards hope. In the vastness of life, the way she makes you feel is a powerful reflection that one person can have a lasting effect on your soul, leaving behind a legacy of strength and resilience.

Through her long-distance healing, Anu Elvis spread good energy and told me a story that made me believe what she was saying. It didn't matter how far away we were because her practices were so warm and healing that they touched my heart. After every healing, I affirmed, "I Gratefully, Thankfully and Happily accept the Healing energies being sent to me".

It was sorcery at it's ….Errrr wait… Na Anu, nopes… The most unexpected exhilaration and power of wellness… I did not need to affirm after every healing, was on Auto-Pilot, accepting the healing energies being sent to me almost throughout the day.

In the field of Positivity, Anuradha Iyer stood out like a bright beacon, showing me the way with her positive light. Her gentle support sparked something in me that made me want to find joy in helping others and be proud of the strength that made my journey unique. The things Anuradha said were a gentle warning in a world full of problems and a call to fight despair.

In my mind, Anu and Anuradha took on the role of emotional builders, shaping the contours of my healing journey. With Anu, the distance wasn't an issue; it was a way for our energies to meet. The emotional resonance of her healing methods became a lifeline for me, weaving lines of hope into my life.

Anuradha's lessons were more than just words; they were emotional turning points in my growth. While problems seemed like storm clouds in the sky, she told me to enjoy the small wins that came my way. The happiness of being alive, which was often overshadowed by the weight of problems, turned into a melody in her voice. It was a lesson that the beauty of life is in savoring every moment.

Like a symphony, my feelings were a mix of gratitude, hope, and newfound power that worked well together. Like alchemists, Anu, Anuradha, and Maria turned doubt into belief and fear into courage in their own special ways.

The friends who were there for me, whether they were physically there or connected with me virtually, are live proof of how strong human bonds can be. Their words of support, their warm visits, and the simple but powerful act of calling me were lifelines for me on my path. They changed into strong threads that woven a safety net under me to keep me from falling into the scary abyss of hopelessness.

The simple act of making a call had a lot of emotional weight. During those times, their words were like a lifeline, connecting our hearts even though we were far apart. A simple question like "How are you?" showed worry and empathy by genuinely wanting to know about my health. Their names are etched in my heart, whether they were spoken or not. They are the notes that make up a beautiful melody in the grand symphony of life. They are the soundtrack that captures the spirit of friendship, resilience, and the unbreakable strength that comes from connecting with other people.

There are threads of shared laughter, the warmth of friendship, and understanding that goes beyond words that run through the tapestry of life. Friends, those dependable company, became my emotional supports, keeping me grounded when things weren't going as planned. Their help wasn't just a lifesaver; it was a liferaft that kept me afloat when things got rough.

I carry these lessons with me like valuable cargo as the trip goes on. You can really feel the power of an upbeat attitude; it's what starts the fire of resilience. With its ups and downs, life's symphony turns into a melody that fits with the pulsing rhythm of living.

So, I want to tell people who are going through similar things not to let the shadows of hopelessness leave a permanent mark on the canvas of your life. Accept life as it is and live it to the best. Let the beauty of your own symphony drown out the doubts. Don't die before you die. Instead, enjoy the bright colours that make up the amazing fabric of your one-of-a-kind, strong life.

As Anu was still undergoing higher qualifications in Pranic Healing, there was a requirement for her to submit a testimony from any of her 'patients' that she had been healing.

I was happy to submit the same.

Testimony for Pranic Healing done by Anu Elvis.

I had been living a very intensive, active and contented life, till about 3 years ago. I was very into a hectic and active state of living. Very involved in my Educational Institution activities and in a networked social life ... again, not very common, at least in those many years back. Did well in my Education, a State Merit list student, School Head Boy, an ardent public speaker and heading & forming Social groups and NGO's at a national level. With such activities and deep involvement, I was gifted with a large number of Friends and very close people. I was very interested in what I could offer back to Society and what I would learn from my close, personal and experienced friends.

This is how I knew Anu Elvis, though many years ago, more as a lady married to a close friend and thus a social acquaintance.

Then the clouds broke and I crash-landed in a few moments. Amidst a very successful and ongoing Global career, Senior Management Globe trotter, I collapsed at the Airport and was shifted midnight to the St. John's Hospital in Bangalore. The Intensive Care Unit (ICU) was my Guest house for almost 10 days, till they figured out what the Medical problem 'seemed' to be... I say 'seemed' to be, as they did not know what, why, how and from when it had started. It's termed as "Sarcodiosis", an anti – immunity problem and to make it unique, after all it was for a special guy like me, it was 'Neuro-Sarcodiosis'. It affected my Neurological system, leaving my body with no scope of any healing possible, in case of any minor health issue, unable to heal even a common cold or cough, leave alone larger potential issues.

Everything was explored and tried. I was provided the best medical care possible, taken to specialty hospitals globally and all forms from Acupuncture, Ayurveda, Acupressure, Mantras, as usual Allopathy topped it all – not to find fault, but this was the only treatment that could be done. 21 tablets in a day, 14 of which were Steroids… every day, without fail. A state level Basketball player like me, gained weight, became dull, bed ridden for prolonged periods, could not walk, often stumbled and fell down, had dementia, tremendous body ache and depression – essentially lost the will to make everyone else around me suffer. Then I was told about Anu Elvis, healing through Pranic. I had always linked Pranic to some sort of specific religious practice, not linked to any reality that I had learnt / was taught about, ever. Reached out to Anu, had hours of talking and she convinced me through sheer practical positivity, explaining the healing, reconciling with myself and accepting that the 'past is past'.. Motivated by her honest clarity, genuine and positive empathy, but refusal to believe that this was 'do-or-die', I WANTED to undergo the Pranic Therapy. Anu started the process, listening to me and discussed asking many questions. It was a sort of a confession to myself, to trust that I might have not realised, but I carried baggage of some guilt related to past, refused to accept that belief could heal me. I agreed and accepted. She listed and sent me affirmations, positive statements that I was to repeat many times, every day. It was 'long distance healing', something that I never believed in ever, but I felt the impact, the energy. Anu sent me "healing done" messages and I was inspired to go down on my knees, thanking the intentions and say the lines of acknowledgement. I experienced a sharp improvement in first my mental my health, sheer energy of goodness, and then physically, incredibly, I started walking around. Initially with a walking stick, more for mental support and Anu applauded that. Once I did that, I was blessed with constant healing sessions and even time dedicated to talking very regularly on phone, to assure that I was enroute to recovery. When certain issues with specific pain in my legs and also depression tendencies, Anu again persisted, kept asking me about them if **"I was being rigid somewhere?? Any area of your life? Reflect"** and focused on her Healing. I acknowledged it and understood. Today, I have started a People Development Consulting unit, as a Certified Life Coach and Mentor. The Pranic healing from Anu Elvis has been so emphatic, I took my First flight in 3 years, just last week and in excitement I blocked a Window Seat to gaze out!! I used to live on flights in my career role, but it had stopped and I never thought I will Fly again. My medicines have come down to 2 steroids and 5 odd vitamins. I conducted a 3 days of Teachers Training in a great Institute of repute and it went great! Anu has been motivating me towards Meditation! Anu Guruji sent me a video link on how to do 'Anulom-vilom Pranayam' and kept following up if I had attempted to start it. I did!! My medically allocated 3 to 6 months of life remaining, has been extended to 4 years now.

It is the ability of Madam Anu to keep it sharp, focused, smart, effective and make it so possible, that has made me a Brand Ambassador for Pranic healing. A post on FaceBook on this healing had incredible number of people responding with a "Binu, tell me more about this" I speak about this Pranic healing experience unabashedly!! Jai Jagat!!

1. Name: Binu Varghese.

2. Occupation : Life Coach and Mentor, People Development Training.

"The Enigmatic Ascent," explains the secrets of a trip on a ladder that serves more than one purpose. As you look at the steps, which are like a wordless story of choices, you might wonder if they lead up or down. Like guardian angels, handrails offer support, which is similar to how

true friends are there for you when life takes unexpected turns. With stories of never-ending support, this journey looks at the deep link between friends and soulmates. A thought-provoking contrast arises: when you have plenty, it makes people wonder and ask 'HOW are you'? and their well-being, while hardship and loneliness make people ask the terrifying question, "WHO are you?" When you change the letters HWO, they form a mysterious question.

Chapter 14
Handrails and Lifelines:

The Role of Friends and Soulmates

As I start this section, after a lot of thinking, I do want to put down these few lines of a personal experience.

As I do so, I do look at that image of the Staircase. Through this experience of mine, it has been Friends, Soulmates, Crushes, Massive empathy with Happiness., yet the next few sentences are real and not alien to many other people who go through the same circumstances.

When I quit my Job with Associated British Foods, the medical environment encompassed me. As I swaggered around, just could not sit still. Had never done so before and could not do so now. Not a Great decision, but I did so. Had been in the food industry throughout my Career and the strings were still here. Of all the things in the

World, Binu Varghese decided to open a Restaurant. Yes, you read that right. Not just a roadside, street food venture, but a full-fledged, High-quality, new trending, Barbeque Grill and Lounge. WAREABOUTS Barbeque Grill and Lounge was born, right at the heart of the high-value real estate City of Bangalore. Taking feedback, to ruin my decision further, got a Vendor with his license to open a Bar on the top floor of the premises.

Great crowds, close Friends, Family associates and the foodies flocked. Quite successful, as indicated when Barbeque Nation opened its new outlet promptly within 6 months and started Business 600 feet away from WAREABOUTS. Had not done it by myself, a Friend, and yet another Friend. "Partners" it seems.

To cut a short story shorter, my Friend Sarcoidosis prevented me from going to the Restaurant regularly.

My partner, Mr. Mnurag Aishra did.

Was told that we were facing a massive loss in terms of our Finances.

Ending this deliberately, without putting down words for the world to see, Ravi came down and looked at the company papers. While in the hospital, a new CA had completed the paperwork and had my approval with thumbprints on legal papers. The deed was done while I was not conscious and approval taken ,from me, agreeing to all the accounts. The financial wizard that Ravi is, he told me, we are shutting this, Tomorrow. To my expressionless look at the hospital, he sort of mentioned " Binu, you have lost One Crore and Forty-Seven Lakhs in this venture".

Amongst the partners, Binu Varghese was the individual who suffered monetary loss.

Some months later, I did notice that Mr. Aishra had a new smaller Restaurant in Bangalore, using the same furniture as what we had, in Ware the Abouts!

In the big adventure of life, we often find ourselves going up and down a ladder-like structure. Imagine a dream ladder made of the threads of choices and decisions, with each step taking us further into the unknown. The journey has both highs and lows, and each climb makes us think about both the next rise and the next descent.

While we're on this emotional roller coaster, feelings are always with us. The excitement of reaching a new height, the fear of what lies ahead, and the anticipation of climbing higher are all strong feelings that make up the fabric of our lives. Our feelings lead us, sometimes following, but always being there, like a delicate dance.

Think about a time when you are about to make a choice that will change your life. People are very excited, and your heart is beating like a drum in your chest. At these times, the ladder seems to go up forever, and you question whether you have the strength to take the next step. Your mind is the battlefield where you fight an emotional tug-of-war between fear and bravery.

Let's explore the descents now. Life doesn't always go up; sometimes it goes down, asking how strong and resilient we are. Think of a time when you are going down and the steps feel harder and more dangerous than ever. A lot of different feelings come up, including anger, sadness, and frustration. WAREABOUTS was done with. These are the times when the ladder's true nature comes out.

Even so, there are places of deep feeling in the descent. Think of the comforting touch of a hand reaching out to help you when you fall, the words that reassure you like a relaxing melody, or the strength that grows inside you as you take the difficult steps. As the journey goes on, these emotional breaks become its heartbeats, telling us that there is light even in the darkest descents.

If you think about life as a ladder, it's not just about going up; it's also about accepting the feelings that come with each step. It's a journey where happiness and sadness, bravery and fear, weave together like threads to make a rich tapestry of memories. So, as you go up, take a moment to feel your feelings' pulse. Then, as you go down, let the emotional symphony lead you through the turns and twists. Emotional colors are what give our lives depth and meaning, after all.

"*You will never gain anyone's approval by begging for it. When you stand confident in your own world, Respect follows.*"

Think of life as a colorful tapestry that is held together by the threads of connections and experiences. In this big plan, think of a moving ladder that goes up to the sky. The strong handrails are like the loyal friends and soulmates who walk with us on this crazy trip. These bars become our steady support as we move up the ladder of life. They're the friends who are wildly happy for us when we win, and their laughing fills our ears like sweet music. When everyone is happy, the ladder seems to sparkle with shared joy, with the marks of shared goals and successes on each step. My classmate Amit Khanna frequently calls me from the US of A and talks to me about my Health and my mom's too. Positivity is what Amit generates. I am a Warehouse of positivity +++ now, am sure.

But life isn't just about going up, like this ladder. Downhill sections make the steps feel shaky and the way ahead is hidden by shadows. When these things happen, the emotional impact of our supports is even stronger. Imagine that your journey takes a turn you didn't expect and you are now facing problems you can't control.

Here, the handrails turn into strong pillars that offer comfort and steady support. Picture a friend reaching out to help you when you're about to trip and fall. Their presence is a sign of comfort. When bad things happen, the emotional link to these handrails becomes a lifeline that keeps you grounded as you ride out life's twists and turns. My classmate Joseph Varghese did that many times. Meetings, Trainings- he would pick me up from home and ignore talking about the challenges that I could face climbing a few Floors or on grounds that were slippery and with ups and downs. Why, Colleen did that last Month and Toolika did that last week! Small town Jabalpur.

Let's look into the feelings that make these times unique. Think about the comfort of a friend's hug when you need it the most, the sound of inspiration that fills the room, and the understanding that goes beyond words. These intense moments are what keep us going and connect us to the people who are riding this life roller coaster with us.

Life is like a big tapestry, and the handrails not only keep us steady but also give our events more depth and meaning. So, as you move up the life ladder, hold on to these emotional handrails. They are the real companions that make the journey worth it, turning every step from ordinary to extraordinary. The person who owns a printing press in Jabalpur, has been doing my work from the time when I was in School and his Dad was running the Press- Taj Printers in Sadar, in front of the Indian Coffee House. Sanjay Kohli continues to look forward to me going to his Press and such huge support, not just professional work, but also actually coming out to hold a hand when I step into his Office.

In this heartfelt chapter, let's delve into the deep and touching influence that friends and soulmates weave into the tapestry of our lives. These extraordinary individuals aren't mere companions; they are the bedrock of enduring support that transforms life's climb into a meaningful journey. Picture this ascent like a challenging mountain, and these companions become the sturdy ropes that help us navigate the steep terrain.

However, the climb is not always smooth. There are moments when the path becomes treacherous, and challenges loom like ominous clouds. It's during these times that the unwavering support of friends and soulmates becomes our refuge. They stand by us, a pillar of strength, ready to face the storms together. The shared burden lightens the load, and the assurance that we are not alone transforms adversity into an opportunity for growth.

Do you have Friends like these? Hand-holding rails on the ladder of life? If you have them, they are not your Friends, they are Soulmates.

As we continue our ascent, the value of these connections becomes even more apparent. The climb is not merely a solitary journey but a collective experience enriched by shared emotions, the tears wiped away, and the laughter that echoes in the valleys. Friends and soulmates, like beacons of light, illuminate the path, turning a challenging climb into a cherished adventure.

In the beautiful fabric of life, friends and soulmates are very important. They keep us grounded when things are going well and we're celebrating. When life is good, when we are full of accomplishments and happiness, and when the world seems full of possibilities, those people are eager to ask, "How are you?"

But when the weather gets dark, the real meaning of these relationships comes out. Imagine a situation where clouds of trouble gather over a once bright scenery. That familiar question takes on a different form and a deeper tone when things are scarce and unclear and the road ahead seems cloudy. It turns into "Who are you?"

It's during these hard times that bonds are really put to the test. Your soulmates and best friends won't leave you; they'll stay by your side. Their care goes deeper than the surface and gets to the heart of who you are. Understanding who you are at your core is more important than what's going on around you. When bad things happen, these emotional moments are like a warm hug in the middle of a cold storm. They comfort and reassure you.

Imagine a friend looking into your eyes, not to find answers to silly questions, but to find out what you're really like. They become a source of support and help you get through the unclear times. It's an understanding that goes beyond words, a shared awareness of the power inside.

The question "Who are you?" becomes an invitation to show your real self, flaws and all, in these hard times. Friends and soulmates give you strength and tell you that your worth isn't based on what other people think of you, but on how genuine your spirit is. As they stand by your side through good times and bad, the friendship grows stronger, showing that real friendships can handle anything and come out better on the other side.

Imagine that you are at the bottom of a steep ladder and that hard times are about to shake your base. These friends and soulmates, who are like steps on your life's ladder, show how strong they really are. Not only should you lend a hand, but you should also become walls of unwavering support. Think about how you feel when a friend looks you in the eyes and asks, "Who are you?" We want to understand you and be there for you, not because we think badly of you.

When things are hard, the tie between friends is like a lifeline. Their help doesn't depend on how well you do or how much money you have. This shows how close they are. They become mental anchors that keep you steady as you go through the storm. Before, the ladder was just a way to get up. Now, each rung represents a shared joy or burden, showing how strong these ties are.

The smart play on letters turns into a moving story about the two sides of friendship. "HWO" is a code that opens the parts of happiness and sadness. "How are you?" and "Who are you?" questions are like threads that are woven into the fabric of friendship. Together, they make a strong tapestry that takes the test of time. You can think of these friends and soulmates as the bars on a ladder—they hold you steady when life gets rough.

Imagine that you are in a situation where you have to deal with a difficult problem. The peak may seem like an impossible job. That next step is easier to take when your trusted friend, or bar, offers their help. Adversity can be turned into a chance to grow when these emotional moments bring the true meaning of these ties to life.

In these stories, as we turn the pages, we read about bonds that last a lifetime. This is a collection of stories about friends who stick together through storms and happy times. In the bad times, remember the laughs you shared with others, which is a sign of how happy you can be when you're with your friends.

Find out what makes someone a true soulmate—someone who can read your heartbeat and dance to it. You can feel these links deep inside, below the surface. True soulmates are there for you when you're feeling weak and need comfort, even when words aren't possible.

With each petal representing a shared burden and each bloom showing the strength that comes from caring for each other, mutual support is like a flower that grows. Imagine that you help a friend when they fall, and they do the same for you when tough times come up. Friendly relationships are like a dance where people give and take, with a tune of support that makes a beautiful symphony.

We learn the deep truth that life is more than just existing until the end, which is inevitable, through these relationships. This song is about loving the people who help us grow, like friends and soulmates. Because we're on this road together, we don't just survive; we thrive.

"In the heart of Jabalpur, I've gone back to my roots and started dancing with fate in a cautious waltz with a walking stick, not because I'm weak but to avoid possible problems. This strange relationship protects against falls and broken bones, making sure that both people can take part in life's grand dance. Jabalpur is a place where people from school, NBS, Navchetana, and other places meet. A tapestry of connections can be seen that goes from Chennai to Goa to Indore to Bangalore to Bhopal to Doha to Dubai to Australia to London to, most famously, Delhi. Life goes on, with and without blessings, and Sarcoidosis is always there, a silent friend with an informally "friendly" relationship. People reading the story are left hanging, wanting to know what other turns and twists will happen in this dance of strength and drive. The stage is set for a truly amazing show."

?

Chapter 15

Embracing Roots, Reconnecting, and Living with Sarcoidosis

Going back to my city of Jabalpur made me feel a lot of different things. The streets whispered memories of my past to me, and seeing familiar faces brought back those memories. It was a meeting with the most important part of my life, a homecoming that made my heart race.

Even as I accepted the things around me that had shaped me, I couldn't ignore the small changes that were happening inside me. "Handicapped" took on a new meaning for me, a truth that came to me like a surprise chapter. Nopes, I wasn't 'handicapped'. Let's get used to the term "limited mobility". Going back to my roots turned into a dance between memories and new challenges. I had no idea the emotional ups and downs that were in store for me.

A simple friend, a walking stick, became a part of who I am. Helping me wasn't enough; it held my fears and the promise of security. At first, people didn't want to depend on it, but over time, they came to see that it was a solid support that wasn't born out of necessity but out of a need for safety.

When she was by herself, in the quiet, the walking stick became a silent witness to her weakness. It reminded me of how thin the line is between being independent and needing help. Each step had an effect not only on the body, but also on the feelings of acceptance.

I kept hearing the experts' advice, which made me think of possible falls and broken bones. The walking stick changed into a guardian, a shield against the fear of having to heal for a long time. Just thinking about being stuck in bed for months on end gave me chills. There was a lot at stake for me emotionally, and the walking stick became the link between my busy life and the scary thought of being unable to move.

At times, the streets, which were once so familiar, felt like they were completely unknown. Emotional weakness and physical pain were woven together to make a fabric of strength. There was a lot of drive in every step, a silent statement that I wouldn't let my situation define me.

As I went through the maze of problems, the walking stick became more than just a physical aid; it became a metaphor for the mental support that helped me move forward. With its friendly people and difficult obstacles, Jabalpur became the setting for a story where the word "handicapped" became a sign of power and determination. Na-limited mobility.

That is where Mannu steps in. Booked a ride, as usual with Ola and got this Auto. To keep this short, but necessary to include Mannu in my Orchestra and the music we played. Mannu and his E-Auto have always been one Phone call away. Anything that he is doing, is completed at the earliest and Mannu is at my gate. Not just the ride, the stop for a shared Tea, or a known vendor for a Samosa is part of our journey.

When I asked him what he does with the couple of Hundreds that he earns from me, he told me "It gets spent the same day". The MD stepped in with a proposal, won't pay you every trip, but will accumulate and pay him Monthly, with a Bonus included. Again, will keep this short, Mannu says it is a life changer for him – he pays his Monthly rent and his Auto EMI, the day it needs to be paid.

Life threw a lot of challenges at me, but finding my way back to my true calling made me feel very at ease. Supporting people's growth was at the heart of my purpose, and it was this love that kept me going even when things were dark. Not just a job, it was a mission that reminded me of how much I wanted to make a difference in the world.

Going back to Jabalpur, a place where fates have been linked, allowed me to meet up with old friends from different parts of my life. From classmates to friends in groups like Navchetana and the Youth group, the connections went far beyond the city limits. It was possible for the links to go through places like Delhi, Chennai, Goa, Indore, Bangalore, Bhopal, Doha, Dubai, Australia, London, and more.

Seeing these faces again brought up a lot of feelings, like a spring of memories. The shared moments, the laughter that echoed down the halls, and the hopes that were nurtured at the same time—it all became a tapestry of memories. Every encounter was like a waltz between the past and the present that made you feel things.

When these places were mentioned, it wasn't just names being said; it was a trip through the landscape of my life. The warm city of Chennai, the relaxed island of Goa, and the busy city of London are all places that hold parts of my story. Each place's emotional impact added layers to my story, making it a collection of events that changed not only me but also the people I met.

Like a never-ending river, life had its own pace. It wasn't just a bunch of facts being dropped; the dance of names and places was a recognition of how life's currents rise and fall. Limitations were like the notes that gave the music depth in this symphony of life. Emotional undertones of strength, facing common problems, and the beauty of getting past them made a clear picture.

As a result, life went on with a rhythm that was strengthened by the times we spent together, the emotional fabric we made across different landscapes, and the knowledge that our paths, no matter how different, had met in the middle of Jabalpur.

While I was making these links, Sarcoidosis slowly but surely became a part of my life. If you could even call it that, our friendship was one of a kind and nothing like "friendly." My sarcoidosis and all of its problems had become a normal part of my daily life. It wasn't what made me who I was, but it did change how I lived my life.

When you had sarcoidosis, you had to accept that it was there but not let it take over. It was like an uninvited guest had moved in, and I chose to share my space with it instead of shooing it away. At those times, feelings came and went like a river. There was anger and discomfort, but there was also an obvious strength that came out in the face of hardship.

Some days, anger was thick in the air, like a storm building over the horizon. The limits that Sarcoidosis put on people would make shadows that could block out the light. Even though they were feeling very upset, there was a quiet resolution that wouldn't go away. Every day showed how strong it is to accept that you have to live with an unwanted partner.

As a steady reminder of the condition, the pain would weave itself into the fabric of daily life. Despite the unease, there were also times when I felt emotionally strong. The small wins, like making it through the day without being too tired or finishing a job that seemed impossible, were like the sun breaking through the clouds.

My feelings about Sarcoidosis went up and down a lot. There were times when I felt hopeless because the weight of my situation seemed impossible to bear. Then, though, there were times of victory, like a phoenix rising from the ashes, which was a sly defiance of the rules that were put in place. There was an emotional tug-of-war going on in the quiet parts of everyday life. It was a dance between being weak and strong.

For this trip, sarcoidosis wasn't just a disease; it was a symbol for strength. It taught me that the human spirit could find a way to grow even when an unwanted guest came along. The emotional scenery, which was made up of both shadows and light, showed how difficult it is to live with a condition and still be brave in life.

The trip was made up of a collage of smiles, mine and those that were already in my life. There may be a problem with names, but life is a tapestry of different events, and each person you meet leaves an indelible mark. Their presence can be felt in every page of my life story, like soft whispers.

Somewhere in the middle of all the ups and downs of life, someone laughed out loud. It kept going back and forth like a melody, an ode to strength and the amazing ability to find joy in hard times. Unfortunately, life went on as usual, and sarcoidosis stayed with them the whole time. But the laughter became a link between the times of lightness in the middle of the darkness.

As smiles were traded, the emotional landscape changed, touching the hearts of everyone around me. These smiles were more than just emotions; they were the links between the parts of my story. Every smile, like a brushstroke painting the picture of shared experiences, told a story of friendship and happiness.

Names were more than just sounds at times; they were the foundations of memories. A person's name wasn't just a bunch of letters thrown out there; it brought up memories of shared laughs, tears, and growth. These people, whose names may come up in the story, helped write my journey and add to the rich tapestry of my life. As life's symphony went on, Sarcoidosis played its own tune, a steady reminder of what it couldn't do. But the laughter became a balance, a tune that got past the problems. It was like emotional alchemy, turning awkward times into chances to share happiness.

I gladly accept the trip, even though it is not perfect and has both good and bad parts. The depth of feeling, shown by smiles and laughter, showed how beautiful acceptance can be. Each smile was a thread in the big fabric of life that told a story of not only surviving but also triumphing over sadness.

Going back to Jabalpur wasn't just a change of scenery; it turned out to be a deep spiritual return, a reunion with the most important thing in my life. That being said, this move wasn't just a change of place; it was a journey of the soul, a return to roots, and an embrace of wings. Once just a tool for support, the walking stick has become a strong symbol of the strength that comes from combining roots and wings on a trip.

As I walked through the streets of Jabalpur again, I realised that this trip wasn't a way to get away from problems; it was a confrontation that would be met with strength and unwavering resolve. Taking each step on these streets became a promise to live each day to the fullest, to help others grow, and to find happiness in the complex web of human relationships.

As I held on to the walking stick, it did more than just keep me steady. It reminded me of the quiet power I gained by accepting how roots and wings are connected. Not only was it bodily support, but it was also a statement of how where I came from and where I want to go are connected. Each step carried the emotional weight of this realisation, a recognition that the coming together of roots and wings is what makes a journey important.

Sarcoidosis is a part of my story, but it wasn't the most important part. With its colors of struggles and victories, the emotional landscape accepted the truth that the condition is a part of my story and not who I am completely. Self-discovery and acceptance were some of the emotional events that led to this understanding.

There were dark sides to these emotional turning points. The problems that Sarcoidosis causes cast their own shadow, but out of the darkness came a strong light. Being self-aware and realising that Sarcoidosis may affect some parts of my trip, it does not control that the whole thing was the light. Acceptance and determination wove together to make an emotional tapestry that showed power in the midst of weakness.

In the bigger picture of my trip back to Jabalpur, the emotional undercurrents were strong, showing that this wasn't just a move, but a deep journey of the heart. Not only were the walking stick, each step, and the challenges that were met with strength part of the story, but they were also a piece of emotional music that echoed what it means to live fully and embrace both roots and wings in the dance of life.

The trip went on, and each step was filled with the sounds of laughter and the warmth of loved ones. I learned the deepest secret to truly living in Jabalpur, where the past and present came together. I am learning to enjoy every moment, challenge, and connection that life has to give.

As I walked along those familiar routes, laughter became the background music, a thread that ran through my whole life. Not only was it a sound, it was a lifesaver and a force that pushed me forward. The deep emotional depth of those shared moments of happiness kept reminding me that life isn't just living; it's fully experiencing.

Each challenge turned into a stepping stone as memories from the past and present came together. Avoiding problems wasn't the point; it was to face them head-on with a strong will. These challenges made me feel things, and those feelings became the colors of my trip, painting it with shades of strength and determination.

It became clear in the middle of Jabalpur that the key to real life is to enjoy every moment as if it were your last, face challenges with courage, and value every connection as a gift. When I made this finding, I felt a mix of gratitude, courage, and the deep joy that comes from embracing life fully.

"Do not judge me by my success. Judge me by how many times I got up when I fell down" – Nelson Mandela

"In the small town of Jabalpur, Binu Varghese, who was a leader in Training for People Development, sparked change by questioning the Caucus's long-held control of leadership roles. The town was full of talk about Binu, the job coach, life coach, and mentor. Instead of taking the plane like he usually does, Binu took a well-planned 7-hour overnight bus ride to Katni, which changed the story. He was greeted by the Principal, Fr. Thankachan Jose, who hugged him deeply and insisted on getting him driven back to Jabalpur. Not a Bus ride for Binu Varghese. This journey was a turning point that hinted at a change in the story and made readers excited for the next part, which would bring unexpected twists and turns for both Binu and the town."

?

Chapter 16
Winning Over Difficulties

When I started my life's journey, I had no idea how many turns and twists it would have. I didn't know that unexpected problems would come up and test the very core of who I am. As I went deeper into the world of People Development and Alternative Leadership, I found a wonderful journey waiting for me. It was a great experience in every place where the plane touched down.

The thrilling success I had in leadership development became the background of my life, a picture of success. Still, Sarcoidosis, a quiet enemy, made its way into my story during the celebrations. It crept in slowly, like a shadow on the colorful fabric of my life. In the middle of my professional rise, this uninvited guest changed the story in a way that changed how I thought about success and performance. I did have simple challenges. Computer education in School in those times was just introduced. I did it and did it well. However, it was the basics. The designation of 'Managing Director' entitled me to Secretaries, who would type as I would request them to do. Even made PowerPoint Presentations- very impressive ones… and now here I was… needing to impress my Trainees and stepped in Haroon Saifee. Another old Aloysian School mate, School times bonding with his Father and him an active member of Navchetana. The bonding continues to this day. Haroon comes often to set up my computer systems and software upgrades and is the Best in town for the work that he does. He owns "Badshah Computers", which is going to be my Office for my latest venture- SUCCESS STATION. A Training, Career Guidance STATION for Superfast and confident careers to be launched. Do check out: www.success-station.in

At the point where success and failure met, my feelings became the threads that held my story together. There were quiet whispers of physical difficulties mixed in with the joy of changing lives and giving communities more power. Sarcoidosis was the bad guy in this complicated story, but no one saw it.

In the middle of my busy work, there were times when I could feel the weight of my Sarcoidosis. A sudden feeling of tiredness and a mild ache are memories of an unwanted visitor. Even though they were physically weak, they showed a strong attitude. Every time they got over one of the obstacles, they cried tears of both pain and joy. The ups and downs of my emotions as I fought an unseen enemy became an important part of my journey.

The effect I used to only measure in terms of professional milestones started to go beyond leadership growth. It went beyond physical wins over pain, staying strong in the face of uncertainty, and being able to see each problem as a chance to grow. My life story wasn't just about job successes anymore; it was also about the human spirit rising above challenges we couldn't see.

Things got more complicated emotionally as the chapters went on. Each win over Sarcoidosis turned into a victory of the heart and a sign of the unbreakable will to get through hard times. Before, the big picture of my life was a success. Now, it's about being strong, not giving up, and finding beauty in the middle of life's unexpected storms.

My hopes and dreams came to life like brushstrokes on a painting in the cute town of Jabalpur, where chances seemed as rare as the dew in the morning. People clung to their places like lifelines in the narrow lanes, unintentionally stunting the growth of the younger generation. The need for alternative leadership development could be heard. My mission as a Career Guide, Life Coach, and Mentor stood out among the noise of leadership talks, giving me the cute nickname "Talk of the Town."

When I chose to cast my net beyond the familiar horizons of Jabalpur and go into the heart of smaller towns, that was the turning point. The road to the even smaller town, Katni, was like a bridge that linked hopes and prospects. It was more than just a trip for me to get on an Inter-City Bus after years; it was a jump of faith. As the bus made its way through the night, the steady hum became the background noise for my thoughts as I thought about the problems that lay ahead.

Going from the busy streets of Jabalpur to the calmer atmosphere of Katni wasn't just a change of scenery; it was also a change in the story of my trip. Feelings were stirring like the bus wheels stirring up dust. There was still some doubt in the air, along with excitement about what was to come. During those quiet times, I began to doubt my choice. When the Bus stopped for a break, Snacks, tea and ... and ... and...and a washroom break. India is most unfriendly for partially enabled persons. Be it Airports or even the Railway Stations, assistance is craven for. I wondered if the unknown areas held the same promise as the areas I had already explored.

But with each mile that went by, a quiet determination grew. There was more to it than just a trip; it was a pilgrimage with a reason. The quiet towns I passed through saw me on my journey, and in their stillness, I heard voices of my own hopes. The problems that were coming up weren't just problems; they were chances to make a difference that would last.

When the bus pulled into Katni, I felt a rush of mixed emotions: fear, excitement, and a strong conviction that this trip could change not only my mission; but also the lives of the people I wanted to inspire. I was invited to St. Paul's Higher Secondary School, Katni, to train Students and Teachers. The interaction and the delivery of the Training was a wonderful flight of execution. What the School wanted. I was invited by the Director, Fr. Thankachan Jose, an ex- Principal of my School, St. Aloysius in Jabalpur. We had an Aloysian bonding, even though he came into Aloysius later than when I had passed out of School. It was Fr. Thankachan's first day in his new assignment in Katni and I was there on his first day in that School. I did have Friends there- there too ?? Yes, there too! Nisha Clayburn was someone who I had grown up with, during our government quarters stay days, in childhood. Nisha is a teacher there. Bonds still do meet Bonds- after years and years. My work went beyond Jabalpur; it was a portrait of strength and drive set against the background of smaller towns and bigger dreams.

It made me feel a lot of different things when I got off the bus in Katni. The director of the school, Fr. Thankachan Jose, greeted me warmly at the bus stop. He had no idea that my body was fighting silent battles inside it. Sarcoidosis had sneakily joined me on my journey, a friend who was making it hard for me to do things physically. What at first glance looked like a simple overnight bus trip turned out to be a difficult job involving both outside and inside forces.

Fr. Thankachan's friendly smile and handshake were more than just actions; they were guiding lights in a storm of doubt. The weight of my physical state was lifted for a moment as real warmth wrapped around me. I found comfort in that brief embrace, a break from the silent battle that had become a normal part of my life.

Sarcoidosis had an effect on my body that could be seen in the form of a walking stick that I had started carrying with me. Each step was a test of my strength and a refusal to give up, even though my body was holding me back. Commuting, which used to be easy, turned into a difficult job, and the familiar ache in my feet kept reminding me of how hard things were for me. Fear of navigating through new areas stayed with me like a shadow that wouldn't go away.

During those times when I felt weak and the physical pain seemed too much to bear, it was the emotional threads that held me together. What pushed me forward was the desire to complete my goal and the burning desire to make a difference. Each step with the walking stick was a quiet statement of determination that the spirit inside was strong, even though the body was hesitantly holding it back.

The trip, which used to be counted in miles, was now told in emotional chapters. Every time they talked or smiled at each other; it gave them strength. Fr. Thankachan Jose, without meaning to, became a symbol of support and a warning that there are people who will stand with you even when you are going through hard times. When I went through Katni's strange terrain, it wasn't just a physical adventure; it was also an emotional one, showing how strong the human spirit can be when things go wrong.

My message of People Development and Alternative Leadership took root in the town of Katni, where chances were few. The problems I had to deal with turned into a blank canvas that my drive and persistence painted on. Even though they didn't have many options, the people of Katni welcomed my goal with open arms. It was his first day in his new assignment as Director of St. Paul's, H.S. School, Katni. I had thought that I was going to attend his Welcome gathering by the school staff. I was momentarily stunned, when he said, you are going to conduct the Teachers Training today. He was the new Director and he had thought of the needs of his staff. I was not carrying my laptop or even a prepared presentation on a memory stick.

As a former Principal of St. Aloysius, Fr. Thankachan knew what could be done. We had a great and wonderful Day, a changed version of me with the Teachers and the Director joining in with his wonderful experience sharing. The bonds with St. Paul's Katni became everlasting. It was rekindled when we were called back to Katni, by Fr. Dominic Thomas, to train young Adults for personal development, bounded by spiritual development. The bonds still persist, with interactions happening almost every week.

As I worked on my project, the emotional impact of my journey grew. Because Fr. Thankachan Jose understood the problems I was having, he did more than his job as school director. His understanding of my problems became a source of comfort and light for me, showing me the way forward. In a kind act, he insisted on making sure of my safe return to Jabalpur by setting up a car and a driver. The kindness he showed me was a powerful lesson that there are people who will stand by us when things get hard.

As I started my journey back, I felt a lot of different feelings. Thanks for Fr. Thankachan's unwavering support and a strong desire to carry out the goal. The car ride, which started out as a way to get somewhere, turned into a trip through the world of kindness and human connection. The emotional ties between Katni and Jabalpur grew stronger in that car, despite the space between them.

It was clear that Sarcoidosis was hard on my body, and every step taken with the walking stick held the weight of both the illness and a strong will. There was a dance between being weak and strong, with a steady beat set by the determination to get through it. Problems with mobility weren't setbacks; they were just stepping stones that helped me move forward in the bigger story of my goal.

The intense experiences in Katni fed my fire, making it burn brighter than ever. The restrictions that Sarcoidosis put in place were like gusts of wind trying to put out the fire, but the purposeful fire kept going. Every time we talked or shared a moment, it made my trip more emotional.

At the end, the emotional victories were more important than the physical fights. Katni, a town that used to be limited by possibilities, became a symbol of how strong people can be. Not only did the steps I took with support tell the story, but so did the emotional ties I made. This showed me that the heart can win even when there are physical problems. The emotional strings were very tightly woven into the tapestry of my life. Each town and City, I went to was like a witness to an inspiring story of determination, where the search for a bigger purpose beat the limitations my health put on me. I was soon in Bhopal, Indore, Hyderabad, Sagar, Begum Ganj (Huh! Where's that?), and in Coaching centers and educational institutions. In Business Offices, Consulting and Training. Personal Counselling was a new phase I entered into. People have problems. People have problems. People have problems. That's deliberately written more than once. People have challenges more than once.

The emotional impact of this trip was felt in quiet but strong ways. With the weight of Sarcoidosis on my shoulders, every step I took was not only an action, but also a sign of how strong I could be. The towns, which were only points on a map before, became live witnesses to a story that went beyond their locations. As the story of my drive and victory unfolded, they became the background.

The emotional turning point came when I realised that the fragility of life didn't make my trip less important; instead, it made every moment more emotionally rich. The simple act of continuing even though they were physically limited became a powerful statement about the human spirit's ability to overcome hardship.

There are more high points- invited to the Xavier Institute of Management Studies, a renowned subsidiary of XLRI Jamshedpur, My Schoolmate, a junior to me, Mr. Vijay Tomar, manager of the Jabalpur division of Amity University insisted that we go to my old College and conduct Personal Development and Career Guidance sessions for the students in my very own landmark point of Life, G.S. College of Commerce studies. What a feeling to step into my College after Thirty-odd years, this time as a Trainer.

The Principal, Dr. Sunil Pahwa welcomed me and gave my introduction to the gathering. So emotional I was, that I insisted ... err... requested for a copy of that Introduction. You have gone through most part so that already, but here it is for Memory's sake:

XXXXX

Principal Dr. Sunil Pahwah, GS College, introduced Mr. Binu Varghese.

Mr. Binu Varghese is born and brought up in Jabalpur. He has completed his Schooling from St. Aloysius, passing out School in 1989, as the School Captain and awarded as the BEST Aloysian Student of the academic term year. He has been a Gold Medal Winner twice, in the National Debating Competition and also a State level

Basketball player. He is Proud to have completed his Graduation and also his Post Graduation, from GS College Jabalpur, where we have gathered today. When he passed out in 1994, we did not have anything like RESUME, atleast in the then small-town Jabalpur. Training Students in " How to attend Interviews, Personality and Soft Skill Developments and Motivational Life Coach Mentoring was a concept in bigger cities like Delhi, Bombay..

Mr. Binu started his Corporate Career with Nestle India Pvt. Ltd, as a Junior Sales Officer, selected for the Job, in his 1st Interview & Group Discussion that he underwent. He went on to grow and stay with Nestle for 11 Years, part of the team that launched Kit Kat Chocolate and as The Brand Manager for Maggi Noodles for India.

After 11 years he moved on to Associated British Foods- Mauri Division, as the Managing Director of 27 Countries in Asia and India. He was reporting to the Global CEO, based in London - UK.

Due to his sudden Health issues, he has come back to his roots in Jabalpur, as An ICF Certified Global Life Coach and Mentor. He is a People's Trainer, a Business Consultant for various Companies Nationally & in Jabalpur coordinating with Happiest Resumes / WhiteForce Placement & out sourcing facilities Nationally, facilitating placements and career guidance. and today he is with us as a Freelance Trainer, aligned with the Amity Team in Jabalpur. Mr. Binu will be speaking to us all, about Career Development, Creating Professional Resumes, and Personality Development. We welcome him as an Alumni of GS College and a Freelance Trainer

XXXXXX

There is another way of my Introduction to my Trainees.

This is the other way that I use to introduce myself. I do it myself, on the PowerPoint Screen – addressing the Students Directly. The reason is that it is me talking to my Trainees, so me introducing myself tuned in a relevant way. Associated with the way that they are and the circumstances of careers and ambitions that my Trainees and me, myself have,

- I AM BINU VARGHESE - BORN AND BROUGHT UP IN JABALPUR.
- SCHOOL CAPTAIN OF MY BATCH IN St. ALOYSIUS
- STATE BASKETBALL PLAYER - NATIONAL DEBATING GOLD MEDAL WINNER TWICE
- STARTED MY CAREER WITH NESTLE INDIA – WORLD'S LARGEST FMCG COMPANY
- IN 11 YEARS WITH NESTLE – BRAND MANAGER OF MAGGI NOODLES – IN THE TEAM THAT LAUNCHED KIT KAT CHOCOLATES IN INDIA.
- WORKED FOR ASSOCIATED BRITISH FOODS- MANAGING DIRECTOR FOR 27 COUNTRIES IN SOUTH & WEST ASIA. HAVE TRAVELLED TO 38 COUNTRIES
- KEYNOTE SPEAKER AT THE WORLD YOUTH DAY, IN DENVER, USA. – 2 LAKH PEOPLE IN THE STADIUM.
- AM A GLOBALLY CERTIFIED LIFE COACH/ MENTOR/ PEOPLE DEVELOPMENT TRAINER.
- MY CTC SALARY WHEN I LEFT THE JOB, DUE TO MEDICAL ISSUES, WAS ONE &&&&&
- AM FROM JABALPUR– JUST LIKE EACH OF YOU HERE.

The CTC point evokes most queries and guesses and I ask them to come personally and ask me about it. And almost each one actually does.

In both busy cities and quiet villages, I came across emotional scenes that stuck with me long after the physical marks were gone. The people whose lives I touch through my goal showed a wide range of emotions, from gratitude and inspiration to maybe a shared understanding of what Young Adults want to grow into – their aspirations, ambitions and the personal challenges they and many times their families face. The towns, with their unique scenery, became the silent characters in a story about how the search for purpose turned problems into chances.

Very importantly, my very own personal experience- of challenges, personal issues, Mom's health circumstances, and possible opportunities that appeared impossible for me, was, and is, the basis of the sharing's that I do in Training and Guiding sessions. Personal Financial challenges always sat in the middle ... hm... left.. .err... right ... of my mind.

As I went on this emotional journey, the places I stopped in weren't just stops along the way; they were parts of a story about strength. Sarcoidosis didn't define my trip; instead, it became a powerful punctuation mark that drew attention to how deeply each physical victory affected me emotionally. It wasn't just about getting to my goal; it was also about the emotional resonances that echoed in the hearts of the people I met along the way.

In the simple beauty of words, life's complicated fabric starts to fall apart. Instead of just talking about Sarcoidosis, this chapter also talks about how to use hardships to grow as a person. It's a story about changing what success means when you have physical limits. The most important thing about it is that it shows how strong the human spirit is and how determined people are to make a difference, no matter what hurdles they face.

The emotional core of this chapter is in every word; it feels like the journey's highs and lows. The human spirit shines even better when it is set against a tough disease like sarcoidosis. When faced with this enemy that can't be seen, strong feelings of courage, resilience, and an unwavering desire to move forward come to the surface.

The simple wording used here was chosen on purpose so that the depths of human experience can be seen. The mental journey that comes with each step is just as important as the physical effects of Sarcoidosis. Every line is like a brushstroke that paints a picture of me not giving up when things get hard, but instead uses those problems as stepping stones to a better future.

The moving scenes in this chapter are meant to touch your heart. A surge of mental strength comes at times of weakness, when physical limitations test the limits of endurance. Not only is it a story about overcoming problems, but it also looks at the feelings that come along with the trip. It's like a symphony of feelings that plays through the story: the lows are valleys full of doubts, and the highs are peaks crowned with victories.

In this chapter, success isn't judged by normal criteria, but by how emotionally rich the story is. That it's about the happiness that comes from small wins, the tears that come from pain, and the strength that people show when things don't look good. People can feel deep feelings through simple language, which takes the reader through the highs and lows of life.

At its core, this chapter is a praise of the human spirit's power to get through hard times. You can feel the journey's heartbeat and connect with the feelings that make each step more than just moving your body. It's the simple language that shows how complicated life is, and it brings out the emotional core of the story, making it a story that speaks to the soul.

? ?

"In a dark room, an experienced counselor dares people to face the problems they face in life by looking at themselves in a strange mirror. The story is clever and wise, stressing that life's puzzles can be "sorted out" instead of fully solved. After that, the story moves on to the problems that young people face, such as financial problems and secret pregnancies. The story hints at a journey that accepts the flaws in life, creating a story that is both mysterious and endlessly interesting."

Chapter 17
Dealing with Problems and Accepting Them

Hey there! In "DON'T DIE BEFORE YOU DIE!", we break down the idea that this book isn't just for people who don't have any problems. If you're someone who thinks life is all sunshine and flowers, take a moment to think about this. Lift your hand, take a moment to notice your happy bubble, and then let's start a trip of reflection.

Think about this: If you stand in front of a mirror, the truth will reflect back at you. Take a deep breath and ask your image, "Are there any problems in your life?" Are you sure?" The mirror turns into a way to learn about yourself and connect with the ups and downs of life. My Dear Reader, Talk to Yourself often, you are the best person you will ever meet.

Dear Friend, life is like a roller coaster ride. There are exciting highs and heartbreaking lows. Our lives are shaped by a symphony of feelings and events. Now, picture for a moment that you don't have any problems or obstacles to get past. It sounds wonderful, doesn't it? Still, our own beliefs often keep us from seeing the truth.

Let's add some feeling to this realization. When did something unexpected happen in your life that left you gasping for air? It could have been a breakup, a failure at work, or a loss in your personal life. Do you remember how your chest hurt and your eyes hurt from crying? Things that go wrong in life are what make us strong, and each problem gives us a new set of emotions to work with.

Now, stand in front of that mirror and think about those sad times again. See the laugh lines and tear scars that have been made. Accept that the person looking back at you is a fighter with a story and a survivor with scars that show strength. Problems you face in life are not obstacles; they are the stepping stones that shape your path.

Who do you think you are kidding when you say your life is trouble-free? Life is a beautiful painting with bright shades of happiness, sadness, love, and pain. We find our power in the lows and our true selves in the highs. Friends, if you thought this book was only for people who were up against impossible odds, you were wrong. For you, riding the roller coaster, feeling every turn and twist, and getting stronger with each chapter.

The path of life is full of problems and difficulties that are a part of being human. But here's the beautiful twist: these problems aren't roadblocks; they're just stepping stones that need to be crossed. Let me take you on a poignant tour of my own life, showing you how the threads of hardship were made into its tapestry.

Think about this: Parents are at a crossroads in their high school student's future and are looking for advice like sailors in uncharted seas. It happens all the time, right? It's funny that a lot of people wait until the water is freezing, until they have to make a choice right away, and until they can feel the pressure. Many of these times, I become a lighthouse of hope by telling my own stories to show options to go forward.

Imagine being in front of a crowd of thousands of people who are all eager to hear what you have to say. That was me when I spoke at World Youth Day in the US. The size of that chance was mind-boggling, and energy was racing through my body as I spoke to the excited crowd. That's a memory that will always be a part of me—a time when problems turned into chances.

Moving on to my job path, I've had a wonderful adventure with Nestle and Associated British Foods (Mauri division). Taking care of several countries and reporting to the global CEO sounds like a dream, doesn't it? But, my friend, dreams are often made in the fire of hardship. There were times when the way seemed hard, making choices felt like a burden, and the future seemed uncertain.

Let's add some feeling to these situations. Think back to a time when life gave you a puzzle and the pieces didn't fit. That's when frustration set in. Now picture how happy you were when you finally put those pieces together and saw a bigger picture. That's the great thing about problems: they're not meant to be solved magically. Instead, they should be dealt with by being strong, determined, and hopeful. Very importantly add 'realistic' to that.

Life isn't about being perfect; it's about being able to handle things that aren't perfect with grace. As you stand at this fork in the road, remember that problems are not dead ends; they are detours that lead to chances you didn't expect. It's in the ups and downs that life's real magic happens.

Think about how much stress a teenager must feel when they don't know how their bills will be paid. Picture a house where the smell of struggle fills the air and making ends meet is a daily fight. It's a fact of life for many young hearts, an emotional weight that makes the happy days of youth seem ancient. Even though things are bad, they keep going, looking for a spark of hope.

Let's talk about a sad moment: a young person dealing with the harsh truth of having an alcoholic father. You can feel the emotional turmoil inside those walls, and the need for a safe and caring presence is overwhelming. It's a terrible fight to love a parent while also being hurt by their addiction. In these times, young people's strength is put to the test, and the search for emotional stability turns into a very deep trip.

Now, let's talk about the changes and turns that life often gives us. When a teen learns that she is pregnant without planning to, it's a time when innocence meets duty. As dreams and the reality of soon to be parents clash inside, it's a tumultuous emotional storm. The story then moves on to show friends who are torn apart but still trying to hold on to the bits of routine in their broken homes.

There is a place for Life Coaches and Mentors in all of these problems. They are there to help people feel better and show them the way through the rough waters of becoming an adult. Think about how being that rock of support and a listening ear in the middle of the chaos could change things. You can't wave a magic wand and solve all problems. Instead, you have to learn the careful art of figuring things out one brave step at a time.

These young hearts are going through hard times that are shaping who they are. They find strength in advice that doesn't promise miracles but knows how beautiful it is to get through hard times with strength and unwavering compassion. Every step of life is like a trip, full of both good and bad things. Problems come up out of the blue, like unwanted guests, and weave themselves into the fabric of our lives. The important thing is not to avoid these problems, but to face them head-on and work towards a solution. Let me give you a clear picture of this truth by using feelings from real life.

Think about the scene: a person is at a crossroads of trouble, facing a task that could crush their spirit. It could be the stress of financial challenges, the memories of a broken relationship, or the deep pain of loss. Even though each problem looks different, they all make us feel the same way: a mix of confusion, fear, and sometimes hope.

Now think about the different stories of two people. One gives up because of all the problems that life throws at them; their shoulders slump under the weight. The mental toll is clear: they feel defeated, and their once-positive spirit is cast in a shadow. On the other hand, picture another person going through the same storm. They stand tall and face problems with unshakable determination. There is a hint of toughness in their eyes.

Let's look at the different forms that problems can take. Think about a time when money problems come up and throw a wrench in your daily routine. There is a lot of uncertainty, maybe even some anxiety, and a constant search for security in this emotional landscape. This chaos does, however, present a chance: a chance to grow stronger through hardship and come out on the other side with greater resiliency.

Now, let's talk about how complicated relationships are. Imagine a heart that is caught up in the complicated mess of a broken relationship, the emotional storm of heartbreak, and the fight to put things behind you. When people are going through tough times, their real strength shines through—whether they give up because of their emotions or find the strength to rebuild.

Remember this when you're facing these different problems: problems don't care what you're going through. No matter your age, gender, or background, they throw their shadows on everyone. Recognizing their presence and getting the strength to get through the storm are the keys. Even though you might not know all the answers, you can get through the tough spots with a little drive and help. When you get to the other side, you'll be stronger for having been through it.

Life is a big picture, so if you're a teenager with big dreams of a successful job, a young person who is worried about money, or a parent who is worried about your child's future, take a moment to look around. Through these roads, you're not going alone. There will be problems along the way, but it's important to know that it's okay to ask for help.

Ask and seek Professional assistance. Machines are made, the way they are made. They will do, what they are designed to do. Human Beings – you and me- are not machines. We are malleable. We can learn. We should learn. Not just in classrooms, but out there in the real world. Get people who have personally experienced challenges. There are many few available. Pick them up. Talk to them. There is a 'code of ethics' that I, as an ICF Certified Coach Follow- "What the Mentee share with a Mentor, remains, just with both of them". The Young person is not a machine, it's a Human who can be trained. Personality Development, Stage fright, Self Confidence levels, nervousness, anxiety- NON-PERFORMANCE- each of these have reasons behind them. They can be identified and tackled.

TACKLE THEM. SOLVE THEM. MOVE AHEAD.

Get Trained. Imagine a teenager who is looking ahead to all the things that could happen and letting their thoughts weave a colorful tapestry of their future. There is a wide range of emotions, from excitement about the possibility of success to fear of the unknown and a burning desire to make a road that leads to their goals. In these times, the need for direction becomes a bright light, a steady hand to help you find your way through the maze of job options.

Now, let's look at a young adult who is caught up in the complicated dance of money problems. Think about the stress of having a lot of bills, having to make ends meet all the time, and the mental strain that comes with it. In this emotional landscape, worry and determination mix, and the search for stability turns into a moving trip. When this happens, admitting that you need help is a brave thing to do and a step towards taking back control of your financial story.

Then there's the worried parent whose eyes are cloudy with fear about their kid's future. Imagine the nights they couldn't sleep and the prayers they said to themselves in the dark. There are strong emotional themes, like the love of a parent mixed with fear of the unknown and the desire to set the child up for a successful and happy future. It's at times like these that getting help and advice becomes an emotional lifesaver, showing how deeply loved families are.

Remember this as you read this chapter: life isn't about avoiding problems. You've had a lot of different situations, and the challenges you've faced have helped shape your story. Problems are not the end of your trip, even if they come in the form of dreams, money problems, or parental worries. They are the bumps and turns that give your story more depth. Accept them, ask for help when you need it, and let them help you grow. It takes a lot of toughness, determination, and a strong will to make your story a true one.

While you're standing at the edge of a huge ocean, waves are crashing against the shore, which represents the difficulties you face in life. As you navigate the rough seas, resilience acts as a steady lighthouse. Coming back from adversity stronger, smarter, and more open to the beauty of life is more than just coming back.

Consider resilience as a secret ability that is just waiting to be used when life throws you a curveball. Imagine a time when the fear, pressure, and insecurity of the world seem too much to bear. This is when resilience comes in like a soothing friend, whispering words of courage and hope.

During a difficult time, do you remember a problem that seemed impossible to solve? It could have been losing a job, or a relationship, or experiencing a decrease in health. Unsung heroes like resilience helped you get back on your feet after being depressed. It's the support of a friend's hug and the voice that tells you, "You are not alone." We become stronger because of those mental experiences.

Think of the strength of perseverance as a lighthouse in the darkest occasions. Although it flickers, it won't go out. The ember is what starts a powerful fire that erases the shadows of doubt and hopelessness.

Remember that resilience is not just an idea; it's your constant partner as you face the unknowns and storms that life may throw at you. Embrace it, take care of it, and let it drive you forward.

Don't forget I was diagnosed with Sarcoidosis. No treatments were possible. Given 'Three to Six Months" to live.

? ?

"Returning to Jabalpur after a global career, I dived into business consulting, starting with the Rajpal Group of Companies led by the charismatic Mr. Shailesh Rajpal. The daily routine of being picked up and dropped back unfolded into a transformative experience. Mr. Shailesh's leadership, personal connections with employees, and commitment to change management became a wellspring of inspiration. Amid the corporate triumphs, the silent battle against Sarcoidosis by Binu Varghese added a poignant layer. The juxtaposition of success and personal struggle created a compelling narrative. As the story unfolds, the reader is left wondering about the surprises and challenges that await in the next chapter, where the intersection of local businesses and global experiences promises a tapestry of unexpected twists and triumphs."

Chapter 18
A CEO's Wisdom: Embracing Change for Growth

Life's unpredictable twists and turns frequently provide us with moments that alter the trajectory of our trip. This is the story of a deep transformation prompted by an unexpected encounter - a trip that tugs at the heartstrings and portrays an image of fresh purpose.

Discover the world of Mr. Shailesh Rajpal, the visionary leader at the helm of the Rajpal Group of Companies. The CEO and the owner. Consider the following scenario: I had just returned to the charming city of Jabalpur and found myself at a crossroads of fate. I had no idea destiny had weaved an incredible chapter for me, ready to open its pages.

Mr. Rajpal's gaze landed on my professional canvas, a canvas that held the imprints of my dreams and experiences in the intricate fabric of life. There was an unconscious connection, an acknowledgment of shared dreams and unrealised potential. The Rajpal Group of companies were into multiple Businesses and the division of WhiteForce was introduced to me. A powerful and impact-carrying Human Resources (HR) company. Mr. Shailesh Rajpal and his Team based in Jabalpur. It seemed as if the cosmos was whispering secrets of opportunity to me, telling me to seize the moment.

Mr. Rajpal offered his hand in professional collaboration and friendship, eliciting strong emotions. A shiver of excitement ran through my veins, like the anticipation of a symphony about to be played. The leap from mere acquaintance to Business Consultant for his revered company was rapid, yet every step was bathed in the hues of promise and opportunity. In the Social media accounts that he holds, the Motto is inspirational. "No rest until you Win".

The emotional undercurrents of this excursion rang out like a beautiful song. Imagine the warmth of gratitude I felt as I embarked on this unexpected journey, the tremendous sense of affirmation - that someone of Mr. Rajpal's caliber believed in my ability. Each activity, formerly routine, suddenly carried the weight of significance, as if I were holding a brush to paint purposeful strokes on the canvas of company strategy.

The friendship that grew between us was more than a business alliance; it was a shared vision, a shared heartbeat that rang in boardroom meetings and coffee breaks alike. Victories were celebrated with genuine warmth that extended beyond the traditional confines of employer-employee interactions. In the months that I spent with the team in his Office, I was given Freedom and liberty to interact with every single employee. Not for a formal few minutes but, many times, hours of one-to-one and small group interactions. Eliciting trust and confidence from the employees to speak out to a Business Consultant, yet a seemingly close person to Mr. Rajpal, had its own challenges. Yet, employees spoke, interacted, and expressed ambitions and challenges. My personal experiences with Nestle and AB Mauri, gave me recognition and confidence to elicit responses from Individuals and team leaders. The wonderful part of this 'Business Consultancy', was the space, respect, and the understanding of the CEO, Mr. Shailesh Rajpal- to listen, accept, and share his own challenges with this Business group and the space and resources accessible to him to make this a truly Global impactful Company. "Great Companies need Great people, that's where we come in" was the creed that was created for WhiteForce- providing Organisations around India, with the required resources of employees, starting with Juniors, Freshers, and Senior Management.

As the adventure progressed, so did the levels of personal and professional growth. Challenges were met not with fear, but with a resilience fostered by mutual trust and respect. It was harmony and mutual acknowledgment of teamwork and new processes implemented.

In the end, this unexpected journey proved the value of recognizing and seizing unexpected possibilities. It emphasized the beauty of a chance meeting, the transformational impact of shared goals, and the emotional resonance that connects our professional attempts to the rich fabric of life.

This phase of my journey isn't just about business ideas; it's a touching story about an extraordinary human relationship that unfolded most unexpectedly. Mr. Rajpal, unlike many other CEOs, opened the door not only to the boardroom but also to a domain where my thoughts might freely dance. His openness to my ideas fostered a collaborative environment, a rare find in the business world.

Imagine standing in front of a leader who not only recognises your worldwide corporate leadership expertise but also values the insights you contribute as a consultant. It was more than just professional esteem; it was an affirmation of the value inherent in each concept, an acknowledgment that struck the very core of my professional identity.

I didn't just travel the corporate corridors during the next three months; I went into the company's heartbeat. As I interacted with each person, I became a listener to their experiences and a witness to the complexities of their everyday tasks. Understanding the pulse of the organization carried an emotional weight, a dedication to embracing the goals and challenges that defined its collective soul.

Consider the situations that occur in the break room, and the emotions revealed in the stories exchanged during casual interactions. It wasn't just about restructuring; it was about recognizing the faces and names behind the company's engine. Each conversation created a link between me and the human fabric that brought the organization to life.

The report I created was more than just a document; it was a tapestry woven with strands of our hopes and promises. It wasn't just a list of suggestions; it was a road plan for positive transformation, a roadmap that contained the whispers of the employees' ambitions. And, in a historic moment, Mr. Rajpal didn't just accept it; he welcomed it with open arms.

Feel the surge of emotion when the CEO, generally sitting atop the corporate pinnacle, not only acknowledged but championed the suggested shift. As we launched on a path towards positive transformation, there was a sense of shared exhilaration, a communal heartbeat of expectancy. It wasn't just a strategy adjustment; it demonstrated the power of a leader who not only envisions but welcomes change with the warmth of genuine conviction. This chapter was a tapestry made with strands of trust, understanding, and the common sentiment of striving for a better tomorrow.

It's not often that you meet a CEO who actively wants things to change in the business world. Most business leaders find comfort in what they know because they're afraid that changing things could throw the careful balance off. But in the case of Mr. Rajpal, a different story emerged—one that taught us the important lesson of accepting change, even when it goes against what we think is right.

Feel the winds of change blowing through your company because Mr. Rajpal, unlike many leaders, saw the need for it to change. It was a surprise, different from how they usually fight change. Imagine the scene where he was in the lead, knowing that the way to progress often means going through unknown territory. It's a powerful lesson for all of us to be open to change and see it as a chance to grow, rather than avoiding it because it might be uncomfortable.

The thing that really makes this CEO stand out, is not just how smart he is at business, but also how much he cares about the people who work for him. Imagine a boss who doesn't work alone in a corner office but walks around with his workers, making it easier for people lower down the ranks to reach out to him. He wasn't just a figurehead during these times; he became someone who listened to concerns, knew goals, and actively looked for solutions.

Feel the emotional impact of this situation: a CEO who breaks the rules and breaks down the walls that usually separate leaders from workers. It's a warning that empathy and connection are not only possible at the top of a company, they're necessary.

Watch the story and picture the times when the leader works together with the workers because he or she really wants things to get better. Being easy to get in touch with wasn't just a show; it was a sign of a leadership style that encourages teamwork and friendship. At those times, the company stopped being just a way to organize things and turned into a community where everyone's voice was heard, every problem was solved, and every success was shared with everyone.

In the end, Mr. Shailesh Rajpal's journey as a leader isn't just a story of how companies change; it's also a story of how accepting change with an open heart can change people. It's a source of motivation for both leaders and workers, pushing them to leave their comfort zones, seek change, and make connections that last beyond job titles and office walls.

Beyond the complicated web of business plans and reorganizing companies, there is a chapter that goes deep into the meaning of human connections. What makes this part of my journey so moving is that Mr. Rajpal really cared about my health, which took our relationship beyond the level of business ties.

Imagine a scene where Mr. Rajpal's care for my health became a guiding light in the middle of a busy business meeting. He didn't just recognize my health problems; he went above and beyond and made personal plans to make sure I was okay. Feel the warmth of emotion in the air as something as simple as setting up food at my seat turned into a deep act of kindness and care.

It was Mr. Rajpal who broke down the barriers that usually keep business relationships from growing in a world where boundaries are common. Here is where the story takes a touching turn: he, a devoted Hindu, and I, a devoted Christian, made a link that went beyond our religious differences. Think about how I felt as he once mentioned that he prays for my health. It rang through my emotions, going beyond the labels we wear. It wasn't just a show of kindness; it was a celebration of how much we all have in common as individuals.

Feel the emotional weight of this situation: a CEO, who usually makes choices for the board, is now taking personal matters into account. In these situations, the business front fell away, showing the heart of real care. The exchange of services wasn't just a transaction; it was a friendship built on empathy and understanding.

Think about how important it was when religious and societal differences stopped being barriers as the story goes on. When Mr. Rajpal did those things, they gave me hope and reminded us that, deep down, we are all the same. This part of the story made me very emotional and showed me that compassion has the power to heal even the biggest wounds.

This chapter isn't just about work milestones in the end; it's also a story filled with feelings and compassion. Mr. Rajpal's care for my well-being became a symbol of how much we are alike as people. It's a story that goes beyond jobs and titles and reminds us that the strongest ties are made through empathy and connection.

This chapter is more than just a business story; it's also a truly emotional story of growth, both for the business and for each person who works there. It's a powerful reminder that success doesn't happen by itself; it grows when people work together and pledge to change. At its core, Mr. Rajpal's leadership goes beyond making money; it's about people, how they grow, and how the organization as a whole succeeds.

You can feel the story's heartbeat as it beats in time with the changes and growth of people. Imagine the emotional scenery that is filled with the bright colours of teamwork, where each person is an important brushstroke that adds to the masterpiece of success. Mr. Rajpal shows himself to be more than just a boss; he is also a guiding force who can lead the ship through the waves of change with a goal that goes beyond the bottom line.

Feelings like a wave of inspiration wash over me as I think about this part. It's not just a story of what happened; it's a motivational symphony that supports the idea that real change comes from people who are strong enough to question norms, accept differences, and put the health and happiness of those around them first. Think about places where the energy of innovation is high and where ideas are not only accepted but also praised as powerful forces for good change.

As the story slowly builds and builds, Mr. Shailesh Rajpal shows that he is more than just a leader; he is also a shining example of deep human relationships. The story isn't just about business meetings and financial records; it shows how one person can change other people's lives. Imagine times when guidance and support are given not only to reach business goals but also to help people grow as people, and this creates an emotional impact that lasts far beyond the office walls. Just last month, when the HR Manager, Mrs. Deepika Sengar, went quite unwell and needed to be admitted to the ICU, Mr. Rajpal kept note of her progress and visited the Hospital. An emotionally taken aback Deepika admitted to the ideal nature of her Boss. This shows even today when an Employee is uncomfortable, Mr. Rajpal needs to talk to them. That connection still remains with me, after more than two years of symphony together.

The team from WhiteForce comes as partners, giving career options to Institutions and persons, trained by yours truly and we are broad-basing the alliance now with partnerships looking at franchises across India for WhiteForce.

This isn't just a story about business success; it's also about how powerful it is when lives are linked. The feelings that run through each page tell us that at its core, leadership is about people and their paths. Mr. Rajpal's story isn't just about business success; it's also about personal growth, links between people, and how one person can have a huge effect on many others' lives.

In the touching story "Don't Die Before You Die," this Chapter stands out as a moving source of ideas. It tells us to be open to change, value diversity, and make links that go beyond work. This chapter isn't just a leadership guide; it's also a reminder of how much we have in common and the amazing chances that come up when we leave our comfort zones.

As the story goes on, you can feel the emotional impact that encourages readers to leave their comfort zones. It's not just lines on a page; it's a call to action that wants people to change the way they think about things so they are more open and accepting. Think about the scenes where characters, inspired by this chapter, go into uncharted waters and learn the beauty of accepting the unknown. Did you think that a Corporate CEO would not do something like this with a Business Consultant and a People Development Trainer? Blessed I am.

The story shows how people grow personally and professionally, and it serves as a reminder that real magic happens when we let change, diversity, and real connections happen in our minds. This Chapter isn't just a chapter; it's an emotional journey that encourages us to live a life full of connections, experiences, and the power to change that comes from accepting the unknown.

As I was concluding this chapter, it was 24th December, 2023. Remember, how we started this Book and the date I was born?

Early Morning, I got this note from Mrs. Deepika, the HR Manager, on behalf of the employees that I had interacted with:

XXXXX

Happy Birthday Binu Sir.

May God continue to bless you and give you all blessings and luck for the many more years to come in your life

Thank you for all your guidance, inspiration, and support through the years.

Sir, you are dedicated and determined in your work. You inspire us to be the best in our work. We feel proud to have a Sir like you.

May you have such an incredibly special birthday that every day afterward starts and ends with love, and Peace of Mind. Happy Birthday Sir

From:-

Deepika Sengar,

HR Manager, Rajpal Group

XXXXXX

It took me 3 minutes to respond:

Dear Deepika and the Team,

Am so proud of being associated with each of you. So Blessed to get this wonderful Birthday wish.

Deepika, working with each of you in our Team, I myself have learnt so much.

Gratitude always,

It's Binu.

When I started to work with alternative leadership, I had to deal with a lot of personal challenges because I was against the established "status quo." Not being hassled, I freely questioned norms in meeting rooms, no matter who the audience was. Back in Jabalpur now as a seasoned Global Professional, I asked sharp questions in groups I was associated with and asked questions that generally people wanted to, but couldn't ask. Sarcoidosis became my silent companion as I did all of my activities, adding another layer to my trip. In the next Chapter, you could be eager to see what new twists and turns, as my close Friend Catherine Mathai told me, about the obstacles of Alternative Leadership.

Chapter 19
Learning to Accept Change

As I began my journey through life, I realised I had a never-ending hunger for something beyond the ordinary, a desire to change. My heart was set on starting a new leadership flame, one that would be a source of hope and a break from the old ways of doing things that kept us stuck. I didn't know that this trip would be full of challenges that would test my strength to the limit.

Coming back home to Jabalpur marked the end of a world business trip, and I felt a strong desire for change afterward. Change, on the other hand, often comes with a lot of problems, especially when it means upsetting familiar habits that have been built up over decades. Change, only when Change is Required. That is my Motto.

Right in the middle of this cute town, my identified requirements for change ran into strong opposition from people who were set on maintaining the status quo. Each time someone tried to bring in a new idea, they were met with resistance from people who stuck to the old ways. Even though there was a lot of disagreement, I kept going because I believed that change, no matter how scary it may be, is the sign of growth.

As the days went by, intense events happened at regular intervals along my path. At times I felt frustrated and like the weight of the obstacles was going to put out the fire inside me. Even so, the light flickered but wouldn't go out even though things were bad. It burned brighter after each setback, creating shadows that told stories of strength. There were many Young Adults who came up, personally though, asking for change. Seeking change. A different way of implementing required actions for people development.

The relationship I built with the people of Jabalpur became an important part of my mental landscape. Their doubt and reluctance were like my own problems. Some of us joined hands and worked through the maze of change together, coming upon our common weaknesses and strengths. Every little win turned into a shared victory that was recognized with a warmth that words couldn't describe.

I learned the power of caring to change things while I was fighting a hard battle. Emotional lines that ran through my interactions helped me understand others better and bridged the gap between their different points of view. "Status quo" wasn't just a refusal to change; it was a web of fears and doubts that needed to be untangled.

With a mix of passion and persistence, this trip changed not only my purpose but also the very nature of leadership. The emotional roller coaster caused a change in me and in a society that had been resistant to change before. As I stood in Jabalpur's changed landscape, the sounds of shared joy and triumph echoed, showing how important it is to be brave enough to question the familiar and welcome the unknown.

I spoke up, not in a quiet way, but in a way that made the meeting rooms where important decisions were being made ring with my voice. In those places of power, I was brave enough to question the established ways and the rules that held us together. I did this in public, in front of everyone, no matter their standing or authority. The road I picked wasn't easy at all. It took me through a place where there was a lot of pushback, and some people even rose up against me. Even though things were hard, I kept going because I was sure that if we don't make changes in ourselves, the winds of change would shape us in ways we might not like. A simple tri-monthly magazine for Jabalpur was the trigger point. The magazine started when I was in High School. I was a writer of a Satirical last-page Article- "Tedhi Muskaan". A Twisted Smile. Still, it was a Smile. 26 years later I came back to find the Magazine still breathes– a single person handling it, even though there was a team, who simply had their names printed in the magazine. The direction for the team was straight – " My Way or the Highway".

Simply asked for more people to be included in the Editorial Board, for the magazine to be more useful. Take people who are professional in writing. To make it useful, for people who "have to" pay to subscribe. Stony silence led to a barge of messages on WhatsApp. Retorts from me were admittedly- STRAIGHT. It ended with a regular meeting of the team turning acrimonious in words and expressions. The responsible designated Head of the Structure dissolved ALL Organizations within 72 hours. That was the first time it had happened in over 40 years.

OBA, the group of Ex- Students of St. Aloysious, another group- another meeting- one more resignation and a polite request to listen to more members. This time adhered to, just like a Senior Aloysian would.

Have taken a back seat for the moment. There are issues to be sorted out.

The designated structural head has disappointed me.

However, common ground brings us to common places and the " Hi's" abound. Most times with a smile added.

Dear Dominic, you have been part of the basic fabric of most of these Organisations. They are of practical utility for young Adults. Are they all doing what they are meant to do?

Since it has been declared publicly that the Individual won't talk to me, you Dominic, please tell the honorable Mr. Reggie David:

" Leadership is a runway. If you don't take off, how will another flight take off ?"

As a Change Management advocate, I helped people find their way through the rough seas of change. That phrase, "If we don't change now, change will change us," became my rallying cry, a steady reminder to embrace the change that was coming. The message was harsh, and it was given with a sincerity that cut through the comfort zone. It wasn't just a message about choice; it was a stark reality that change wasn't just an option but a must for life.

As the drama of organizational change played out, emotional events colored my trip. There were times when the weight of resistance felt like it could break the heart. At that time, I held on to the hope that people who seemed hostile actually had a deep fear of the unknown, a fear that, when met with understanding, could turn into a drive to work together.

In the ongoing fight for change, I came across doubters and opponents, each with their own unique way of opposing the coming change. I kept going, though, not just as a sign of change but also as a light of hope. It was clear that this project was hard on many emotions, but through the shared battle, new bonds have been formed. Every problem that had to be solved was a chance to connect on a personal level and help people see things from different points of view with understanding and kindness.

In the middle of this difficult journey, I found the emotional fuel that kept me going: the shared stories of people who had overcome hardship and the unspoken unity among those who were brave enough to question the status quo. Not only did the trip change things, but it also changed people's minds and hearts.

So, as I stood in the changing landscape, the emotional memories of my trip remained. They were a reminder of how resilience, empathy, and the courage to face change head-on can change your life. It wasn't just a journey through organizational change; it was also a trip through the core of human resilience and the opportunity for groups to change.

As I stepped into this new world, I found my place among people of different backgrounds. But I wasn't just watching; I was actively involved by asking questions that spoke to the wishes many people had but were afraid to say out loud. In the end, I became the voice for the silent, an advocate for those who wanted change but didn't have the guts to say so.

I took on the jobs of mentor and trainer for a group of lively young adults during these events. I saw untapped promise in them—a hidden ability to carry the torch of change into the future. I wanted to raise the next generation to be change agents, so I took it upon myself to teach and care for them. Not only did they promise to change the present, but they also promised to shape a better and more exciting future.

In the quiet times when people shared their hopes and goals, this journey's emotional threads began to emerge. At times, fear set in because the weight of unspoken wishes seemed like it would drown the spark of hope. At that time, I was like a lighthouse, showing everyone how to accept their goals with the knowledge that change is both inevitable and a force that can be used for the good of all.

As the trainer and mentor, one time termed as a 'dalaI' (broker) saw how support and direction can change things. Some of the young people I mentored had "aha!" times when they realized how much potential they had. Not only were they learning new skills, but they were also learning to believe in themselves and know that they could change their lives.

So, as I watched this story develop, I felt a sense of empowerment and change that stayed. It was a reminder of how strength can come from working together and how resilience can come from having the same dreams. It wasn't just a trip through unknown territory; it was also a trip that gave people hope and bravery and set the stage for a generation ready to accept and lead change.

As I reached out to different people and connected with people from all walks of life, I was unexpectedly accompanied by sarcoidosis. It was more than just a health problem; it was a constant reminder of how fragile life is, an unwanted partner who taught me deep lessons about being strong and how precious every moment is.

Travelling did take its toll on my emotions. There were times when personal problems were linked to the larger goal of bringing about good change. The strength that Sarcoidosis had given me helped me through those times. That strength told me, "You can weather this storm; you've weathered storms before."

The link between my own problems and the bigger story of change became impossible to break. Once an unwelcome guest, sarcoidosis has changed into a sign of power and a silent ally in the fight for a better world. During the quiet times of reflection, when life seemed fragile and people were determined to make a difference, the emotional impact of this trip could be felt.

In the chaos of everyday life, I found a deep truth: change is not a lofty lecture, it's a melody that needs to be danced to. It tells us to leave the things we know and jump out of our comfortable homes into the great unknown. Even though this discovery is scary, it beats with a vitality that can't be ignored.

Imagine a sheet painted with shades of doubt, with each stroke a sign of the change I was about to go through. The emotional peak of this change was shown in detailed scenes, like a sad melody building up in the background. There were times when I was nervous and afraid of what was beyond the edges of what I knew. Along with the fear, there was a soft thrill: the thrill of anticipation, of what could be won by going into the unknown.

Among the many changes that were happening, I found myself asking questions that kept going through my mind. I could feel the impact on my personal life too. There is mom, bedridden for more than a year, Dementia, Parkinsons – did Sarcoidosis have a larger unplanned family of goons on a roll? You could feel the emotional weight of those questions in the air, like storm clouds that are about to rain. What if what we think we know is just a cozy illusion? What if the real meaning of life is outside of the limits of our everyday lives? Even though these questions were upsetting, they led to a big change in viewpoint.

As I learned to handle the rough waters of change, I realized how important it is to get other people to join the dance. As we took each step, a wave of empathy went through us, reminding us that we were not alone as dancers but, as a group moving to the beat of change. Sharing personal experiences brought people together in ways that words alone couldn't.

In the middle of this complicated dance, training became a key part. As I led the next generation through the complicated steps of change, I saw the light bulb go off in their eyes. It was a deep link, an emotional link between the past and the future, like passing a light that was on fire with the passion of evolution.

The music of change was led by time, which never stopped. Every moment, like a valuable note, held the potential to be a masterpiece. When I came to this realization, it made me feel very sad and made me want to take every quick chance to make a change.

This part of my life wasn't just a call for change; it was more like a mental journey. It was an adventure full of both fear and excitement, a dance of understanding and shared experiences, and a mentorship that felt like it was giving and receiving knowledge. The constant ticking of life's clock made me feel even more emotionally rushed, telling me that every heartbeat is a chance to leave an indelible mark on the constantly changing canvas of existence.

As we embark on the unpredictable journey of change, let's etch this easy truth into our hearts: Perform before you truly live. Feel the beat of life and let it infuse you. As we set sail for uncharted waters, fear and joy are stirring within us. Imagine standing on the edge of the unknown with your heart racing with fear and excitement.

Feel the chill of doubt, like a breeze that raises your hair and makes you shiver. Moments of pain are where resilience is born. Face the difficulties with the same enthusiasm you would for an old friend, because each handshake is an opportunity to grow. Thinking of the way ahead not as a scary maze, but as a road lit by the sun that will make you feel warm after the storm.

Combining bravery and weakness is needed to lead this mission. Imagine the emotional scene where hope and determination meet. Everyone's ability to change, learn, and grow is shown by every step forward. Therefore, let's not just live during this time of change; let's thrive. At these emotional levels, the symphony of a better, more fulfilling future plays its most beautiful sounds.

"You will never be perfect, but you will always be adequate" – Trevor.

A room full of trainees participated in a unique self-discovery activity. We didn't use the usual SWOT analysis; instead, we used the fun ABCD method. People were getting more and more interested as I listed my chosen traits from A to Z, from being Authentic to Vibrant. The surprise turn of events happened when S, who usually stands for Sarcoidiosis, refused to be the center of attention at that time. There was a pause in the conversation, and the trainees were on the edge of their seats, wanting more. They will never forget the story of self-discovery told through the letters of positive traits. It made them eager for the next exciting part of this amazing trip.

Chapter 20
Defying the Shadows

Sarcoidiosis is a disease. "Neuro Sarcoidiosis" is worse. A scary whisper that travels through my mind like an unwanted guest that won't leave. I've made up my mind, though, that this scary word will not have any control over the story of my life, no matter what shadows it throws. Allow me to take you on a trip through the unwritten pages of this chapter to find out how I'm taking back control of my life by combining brave and vulnerable moments.

Life, being a great writer, often mixes surprises with hard situations. For some of us, those difficulties come in the form of a mysterious word that sounds strange when we speak it. Introducing Sarcoidiosis, a word that has suddenly appeared in my vocabulary. But within the syllables of this scary word, I find the power to change the way my story goes. Picking up the pen and not letting this word be the main character in my story is a choice.

Imagine this: a tragic moment when I don't know what's going on and the weight of a diagnosis rests like an anchor in the depths of my soul. An internal storm of emotions swirls as I try to deal with the truth of living life with this unexpected companion, Sarcoidiosis. Within the storm, there is a flicker of rebellion, a spark that won't go out.

There are bright days when laughing sounds like music and quiet nights when I feel like I'm walking through a familiar fog. Families and friends who have always been there for me stand by my side, their love a healing balm for the gaps I can't see. There is strength in their eyes, and comfort in their hug. Finding myself on the less-traveled path leads to times of reflection that make me realize how fragile life is. Even though it's just the sun going down, a sunset is a beautiful display of fleeting beauty that reminds us to savor every moment. Everything becomes special, and every heartbeat shows how strong you are.

Although Sarcoidiosis is a strong enemy, it will not be in charge of conducting my music. I've decided to write a melody and fusion of vulnerability, and unwavering determination in the face of doubt. This chapter isn't defined by a single word; it's a song of strength and a testament to the unbreakable spirit that won't be controlled.

What does it really mean to fight death before it takes us? It's about-facing problems with unshakable determination, even when they seem like they can't be solved. It means finding your inner power, being able to deal with problems with a strong will, and seeing the extraordinary in the everyday details of life. Sarcoidiosis is always there, like a ghost in the dark, but I've decided not to let it change the focus of my life. So, I've decided to turn my attention to the things that give life meaning and color. Let me talk about the inner events that gave this choice life.

Imagine a time when you feel weak and realize in silence that life has thrown you a surprise strike. Sarcoidiosis comes into the picture and is felt like a sudden chill in the air. At that point, you can either give in to your fear or rise above it. If you choose to be resilient, you'll feel a sense of emotional success that is stronger than the whispers of doubt.

As the tides of daily life change, I've learned that the beauty of life is not in big acts of kindness, but in small acts of joy. When people you care about laugh, it sounds like music and drowns out the dissonance of fear. A smile shared or a touch that makes you feel better are the emotional threads that connect people and keep them warm when bad things happen.

Sarcoidiosis may be an unwanted friend, but I'm not going to let it hide the beautiful colours of life. Every sunrise has an emotion that colours the sky with shades of hope. It's like a quiet thank you that every dawn is a gift. The soft rustling of leaves is a moving reminder that life's flow stays the same even when things get hard. The beauty of this trip is not in denying it, but in accepting it: that life is a mosaic of highs and lows, and that every moment, no matter how big or small, adds to the whole.

Looking for comfort in the arms of loved ones, where feelings speak louder than words, is what the story is about.

So, to not die before I die means to enjoy the variety of life, to feel the emotions that flow through every heartbeat, and to let the essence of being alive fill the canvas with a wide range of events. In the face of Sarcoidiosis, I decided to live, and when I did, my emotions became the vivid brushstrokes that painted a picture of strength and joy.

I've learned along the way that having a positive attitude can give you a lot of power. It's not just a thought; it's a wall that keeps bad things from getting in. Every day is like a painting; the bright colors of hope add life to what might otherwise be a dull scene. When things are begging you to give up, choosing hope is an emotional victory.

Take a look at the emotional scenery of a day, when the sun comes up and makes everything warm. Sunshine isn't just a color; it's an image for the choice to be positive. The rays shine on the road and get rid of the shadows that look like they might swallow it up. It's a real example of how choosing to be positive can bring you inner light when things go wrong.

That's when the power of a good attitude really shines through: when the world is quiet and peaceful. There is a voice that says, "You are greater than this." The problems you face don't make up your story. Finding out that there is a light inside that won't go out, even though there are clouds, is an emotional awakening. So, life is like a canvas that is painted with feelings of strength, hope, and an unwavering desire to write a story that goes beyond the limits of a medical diagnosis. Even though I have Sarcoidiosis --nopes -- "Neuro Sarcoidiosis", I have decided not only to live but to live with a spirit that shines with the emotional brilliance of strength and hope.

There is a weight that I carry in the quiet times when the medically untreatable weighs on me, but I've learned how to carry it with grace. It's a part of my journey that I don't want to be there, but it's not the one setting the direction. Accepting my weaknesses has made me stronger, and during these emotional times, I've learned how important it is to lean on others for support.

At the heart of this journey's emotions is a deep lesson in being strong. Not denying the opponent exists, is not the point. The point is NOT letting the opponent set the rules. The emotional backbone is a support system made up of people who understand and care about you. People who share smiles and tears form a link that can't be put into words. Sarcoidiosis is a heavyweight competitor, but it can still be defeated. The Six months to live allotted to me has been left behind. Realizing that the battlefield is more than just the physical world; it also includes mental and emotional strength is an emotional shift. Every morning, sunrise is a sign of new strength, and every evening, sunset is a reminder of how strong you were all day.

For people who are going through their own battles, whether they have Sarcoidiosis or another problem, the lesson is clear: don't let the problems define you. Let your decisions and actions instead become the stories that define you. This is an emotional call to live fully, to enjoy the journey with all of its ups and downs, and to not let the dark sides of hardship dim your spirit.

It's not just a statement; this message is an emotional plea to be strong when things get hard, to find joy in the everyday, and to believe that the story doesn't stop with a diagnosis but continues with chapters of growth, resilience, and surprises.

I trust that I have dug in the word "Sarcoidiosis" in everyone's mind reading this Book. It was deliberate. Very deliberate. Smile if you haven't head of that before. I didn't ever.

I got Seven of my Friends- the close ones- to put in words that define Binu Varghese, for them. A common exercise I do in my Training Programs for People Development at my, Training Organisation- Binu's SUCCESS STATION.

We put my traits in order:

A - Authentic In a world full of facades, I chose to be authentic. Being true to oneself, embracing imperfections, and standing firm in my beliefs became the cornerstone of my character.

B - Blessed Recognizing the abundance in my life, I embraced gratitude for the blessings, big and small. This mindset transformed challenges into opportunities and setbacks into lessons.

C - Confident Confidence is not about being loud; it's about trusting oneself. I cultivated confidence to face uncertainties, knowing that belief in my abilities would guide me through.

D - Determined In the face of obstacles, determination fueled my journey. I adopted a never-give-up attitude, turning setbacks into stepping stones toward success.

E - Empathetic Understanding other's feelings became a strength. Empathy opened doors to meaningful connections and collaborations, fostering a supportive environment.

F - Focused Amid distractions, staying focused on goals became crucial. It required discipline and prioritization, ensuring that my energy was invested in what truly mattered.

G - Grateful Gratitude isn't just a practice; it's a way of life. Being thankful for experiences, relationships, and even challenges brought immense joy and contentment.

H - Hopeful Maintaining hope, even in challenging times, became my guiding light. It propelled me forward, reminding me that every dawn follows the darkest night.

I - Insightful Seeking deeper understanding allowed me to navigate complexities with clarity. Insights became the lanterns illuminating the growth path.

J - Just Fairness and justice formed the foundation of my actions. Upholding principles and treating others with equity became non-negotiable.

K - Kind-hearted, Knowledgeable Combining kindness with knowledge, I aimed to contribute positively to others' lives. A compassionate heart coupled with continuous learning opened doors to meaningful connections.

L - Loving Love is a powerful force. Cultivating love in my interactions fostered an environment of warmth and acceptance.

M - Mindful Living in the present moment, being mindful of thoughts and actions, allowed me to savor life's beauty and navigate challenges with grace.

N - Naughty A touch of playfulness kept life vibrant. Embracing the inner child and finding joy in simple pleasures added a delightful flavor to my journey.

O - Original Unapologetically being myself, embracing uniqueness, and avoiding conformity allowed me to shine authentically.

P - Perseverant Endurance in the face of adversity defined my journey. Perseverance became the bridge between dreams and reality.

Q - Quick Responding promptly to opportunities and challenges, being quick on my feet, enabled me to adapt and thrive in a dynamic world.

R - Resilient Bouncing back from setbacks with newfound strength, resilience became a testament to the human spirit's remarkable ability to overcome.

S - Soulful Connecting with the depth of my soul and embracing spirituality added meaning to my existence.

T - Thoughtful Considering the impact of my actions on others became a habit. Thoughtfulness created a ripple effect of kindness and consideration.

U - Understanding Seeking to understand before being understood became a mantra. Compassionate listening and empathy bridged gaps and strengthened relationships.

V - Vibrant Infusing vitality and energy into every endeavor, I chose to be vibrant in my approach to life.

W - Warm-hearted A warm heart radiates kindness. Fostering genuine connections and spreading warmth enriched my life's tapestry.

X - Xenial Welcoming strangers with hospitality, I embraced the spirit of xeniality, fostering a sense of community wherever I went.

Y - Young Maintaining a youthful spirit, I refused to let age define my curiosity, enthusiasm, and zest for life.

Z - Zealous Approaching life with passion, I remained zealous in pursuing dreams and embracing the journey with excitement.

Adjd569764464sjfiud ----Come on, admit it, you were too lazy to read that text.

Dear Reader, admittedly, I will not be 'Beautified' as a Saint, after you read the traits identified as mine. You are most welcome to disagree yet the idea is to build yourself. Learn. Practice. Make it a habit. Grow. SUCCEED.

Dear Reader of this Book- you put your own Traits – in the same order as I do. Try it.

It's Binu asking you to do so.

In the final pages, Sarcoidiosis may linger, but it's not the lead character in my story. I am the protagonist, navigating the twists of the plot and emerging stronger with every turn. This is a tale of resilience, a journey where I choose life over despair, refusing to let any condition dictate the terms of my existence. You can too.

Imagine a moment where Sarcoidiosis tries to take center stage. The emotional weight is palpable, a test of the hero within. It's a choice between surrendering to despair or finding the strength to rise above. In this pivotal emotional juncture, there's a quiet determination that echoes, an affirmation that the hero's journey is defined by resilience and the refusal to let circumstances dictate the narrative.

This story is an emotional odyssey, where each chapter becomes a testament to the triumph of the human spirit.

Now, imagine walking through the pages of this narrative, where every step is infused with the emotional weight of a choice. It's not just a journey; it's an emotional pilgrimage, a testament to your resolve to live with purpose and resilience. Friends and loved ones become emotional companions, their support a guiding light in the darkest corners of the plot.

In extending an invitation to join me on this journey, there's an emotional plea. Life, a celebration meant to be lived fully, becomes a rallying cry against the shadows. Sarcoidiosis, though present, is not an impediment but a backdrop to a unique celebration of courage and hope. It's an emotional defiance, a refusal to let anything hinder the joyous celebration of existence.

Together, let's defy the shadows that threaten to dim the brightness of our spirits. The invitation is not just a gesture; it's an emotional call to co-author a story that is uniquely ours. It's a narrative woven with threads of courage, hope, and the indomitable triumph of the human spirit—an emotional saga that resounds with the melody of resilience and the celebration of life.

" *You have to fight the fight, to win the fight* " --- Graham Swiss

! ! ! ! !

"When the normal pattern doesn't work out, we need to look at things differently," says a mysterious person who shakes up the world of settled routines. Individuals don't want to change because they are comfortable with their habits, but organizations are happy to take on the task. "Change Management—only where it is required, has been my Principle in Life" is recited by a rebel who lives by this principle. There is a chain reaction of change that starts when the rebel breaks up the harmony of security. What happens next will be an interesting trip into the unknown, with lots of exciting things to look forward to.

Chapter 21
Make Peace with the Rebel inside you.

'Rebel' is not exactly the word that I have in mind to use, in this Chapter. Yet...

Life is funny how it can throw us curveballs, isn't it? Just picture yourself stuck in the boring flow of daily life, doing the same things over and over again. What you know and what you can count on makes you feel better. Walking down a road you know like the back of your hand is a lot like that. Then, out of the blue, life changes everything.

You are enjoying your comfort zone when all of a sudden, the ground starts to give way. It's kind of like standing on unstable ground; everything you thought was safe starts to fall apart. Simply put, it's confusing. You want something more, something different, because your routine, which used to make you feel safe, now feels like a cage.

Now that things are changing so quickly, feelings are running wild. Feelings of being open to the unknowns that life brings us make us feel vulnerable. Feelings of fear start to take over your mind. Here's the thing, though: it's exactly when things are going badly that the 'rebel' in us needs to come out.

Think of this 'rebel' as a lighthouse of hope, a spark of defiance against life's storms. Breaking free from habit and welcoming the unknown with open arms is what it's all about. It's scary, but your rebellious spirit tells you that this is your chance to change the story. Fear, doubt, and the thrill of going into the unknown make it an emotional roller ride.

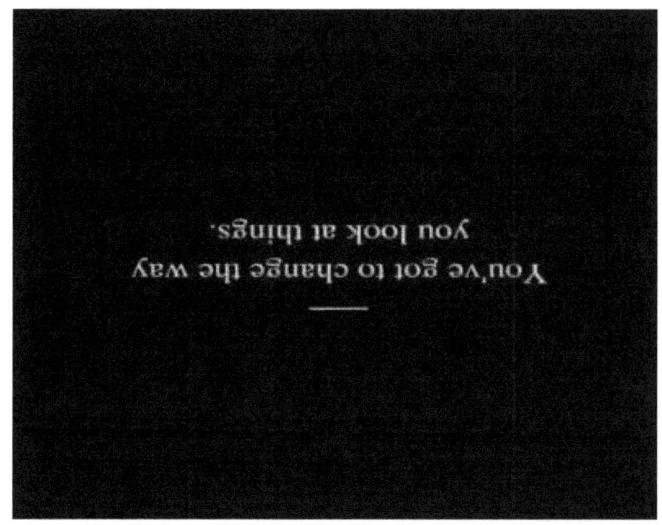

Yes, we need to often look at things differently. Many times, but not all the time. What do you do now? You change your story so that you are a 'rebel'. You find the guts to take a risk and question the way things are. That's not about being careless; that's about being strong. You get strong when you're weak and brave when things are crazy. In the middle of it all, there's beauty in finding your own hidden sources of power.

Life doesn't always go as planned, but that's where the 'rebel' paints his or her work. You change the story with every brave move and every step into the unknown. In times of trouble, it's not enough just to survive; you have to thrive.

As you stand there in the middle of the chaos and your feelings, you realize that being a rebel isn't just resisting because you want to. Accepting change, growing from pain, and letting your feelings lead you through life's unknown seas are what this book is about. When things don't go as planned, be the rebel who rises from the ashes, making a song of feelings and strength that will play through your life. Usage of the word rebel is deliberate here.

Think of a group of people, each managing the maze of life and facing problems that seem impossible to solve. No one is more familiar with this scene than people stuck in a cycle of habit that makes them feel safe. But what happens when safety turns into paralysis?

While working with both groups and people, I've noticed an interesting trend. When dealing with problems, people often cling tightly to what they know, even if it's clear that the current method isn't working. Watching someone hold on to a broken umbrella in a storm because they're afraid to accept change is horrible. "Status Quo" is the term of the time.

People who are feeling this unwillingness to leave their comfort zone are usually the ones who have the hardest time with this idea. People are emotionally connected to their routines, and they are afraid of what the future holds. Instead of just doing what they always do, they don't want to upset the balance they've carefully created, even if that balance is on the verge of not working anymore.

Imagine yourself standing in front of these people and requesting/ asking/ speaking out to them, telling them to change things and question the status quo. People are clearly against the idea of change; they can feel the pushback. The emotional trip starts here, though. Despite their resistance, there are moments of weakness, like doubtful glances in their eyes that hint that the road they are on might not be the best one.

NOBODY IS PERFECT !

I AM NOBODY !!

Balance is needed between what you know and what you don't know. For example, the fear of failing and the anxiety of going into uncharted area are big emotions. Although these feelings are connected to the chance to grow, for a trip that changes you and takes you to new heights.

This idea seems more reasonable to organizations, though. Others agree that sometimes breaking the rules is what leads to new ideas and growth. A lot of people have come to the conclusion that the apple cart sometimes needs a soft push or a firm shake.

Ultimately, it's about discovering the balance between the security of habit and the untapped potential that lies beyond it. There is a lot of mental tension between the safety of the known and the excitement of the unknown. Consider this when you're facing problems: maybe, just maybe, upsetting the apple cart is the emotional and life-changing trip you need to take.

Accepting change has become my way of managing life. But the most important thing is to know when change is necessary. Imagine an engine that is well-oiled and running happily. Why break up the peace at that time? It's like adding more fuel to a machine that's already working well; it adds extra work that isn't needed.

But there are times when change is not only an option, it's the only way to stay relevant. Imagine a group of people who are working hard to solve problems. You can feel the stress in the air. As doubt grows, the emotional pulse quickens. In this case, change isn't just an idea; it's a real need to fix what's wrong.

Emotions are easy to miss when they're buried in the quiet of daily life. But when things need to change, they do: fear, joy, and hesitancy. As you go from the safety of the known to the unknown, your emotions will go up and down like a roller coaster.

So, my guiding concept is still the same: make changes for the better, adapt when necessary, and understand how others feel. Life's changes aren't just mechanical tweaks; they're the emotional crescendo that gives the melody more meaning.

Now, let me share a story that illustrates this point.

There was a time when the fate of a community in a small town was tied to the rhythm of traditional farming. Their fields had been the source of food for a long time. They were tilled with the same care and planted with known seeds. The seasons moved in a steady rhythm until the day shadows covered the once-bustling town. The town was having a hard time because the crops, which used to be plentiful, started to get smaller.

During this sad time, a rebel stepped forward—someone who wasn't afraid to go against the rules. Instead of the tried-and-true, the rebel suggested a new music for the fields. People in the community were feeling very emotional. Things that were known were being tested, and uncertainty cast a long shadow. People are often afraid of change, especially when the known is being traded for the unknown. This made the rebel face opposition.

Still, the rebel kept going because of a belief that went beyond defiance. It was an appeal to adapt and accept change, not just for the sake of trying something new, but so that the community could keep its core. This trip was full of different emotions: anger and fear mixed with the rebel's unwavering resolve. It was an uphill battle against the weight of custom and a powerful reminder that the way to renewal is often through emotional turmoil.

The change happened with the changing of the seasons. Gradually but surely, the neighborhood saw a change. When the rebel played an unusual tune, the fields moved, which they hadn't done before. As the crops did well and brought new life to the town, people cried tears of joy and smiled with hope.

Imagine that this story is echoing through the halls of your problems. Regular fixes don't always work, whether it's at work, in relationships, or inside yourself. At those times, you get stuck in a boring pattern. At this very moment, there are strong feelings present: anger and maybe even hopelessness. In this story of your life, what do you decide to do? Will you be brave like the rebel and question the status quo, knowing that change isn't always a bad thing, it's what will make you thrive?

Let out your inner rebel, and let's read a story about growth and change.

Imagine a world where people question the rules, break the routines, and accept and even embrace change. Imagine a place where people don't fear being uncomfortable and instead see it as a chance to grow as individuals and as a group. It's not about being careless; it's about having the guts to upset the status quo when it looks like things are about to get stuck.

At the center of this story is a rebellious figure who has the guts to question the way things are. Feel the feelings that are going through this rebel: the fear before taking the first step, the drive to keep going in a different direction. Change isn't just an idea; it's an emotional journey that can be scary, exciting, and everything in between.

Our rebel teaches us that change management isn't about making things worse just because they're different. It takes skill and strategy to figure out where change is the key to growth. Imagine the emotional fight that's going on inside: the fear of leaving what's familiar and the excitement of what's unknown. Finding your way between the known and the unknown is like walking on thin air.

Finding the right time to add more fuel to the engine of life is what the story is all about. When things are going well, feelings like happiness, thanks, and maybe even a little fear that it won't last grow. But our 'rebel' says, "Why not embrace change if it can make the good, even stronger?"

Now, think about your own path. Picture yourself facing problems and feeling the weight of routine pulling you down. There is an emotional current going through it—frustration and maybe a touch of acceptance. "Embrace the Rebel Within" is what is my call to you. People are being asked to think about problems in a new way, to be open to change and to not be afraid to upset the apple cart if it will lead to a better harvest in the end.

Because, in the big picture of life, the goal isn't just to stay alive; it's to thrive and make a life that has meaning. So, let your inner rebel lead you, because the patchwork of a life worth remembering lies in the pain of change.

" If plan A didn't work, the Alphabets have Twenty-Five other letters"

?

"My life started a new chapter in Jabalpur after my dad suddenly left us in Bangalore. Later, Mom's health problems made things even harder. With the coming of my sister Binza and her husband Ravi, we said goodbye to Dad and had to deal with the fact that we had to take care of Mom. Upon my return to Jabalpur, I managed to get through life using a walking stick (Support system?) and 14 steroids every single day, finding comfort in the sidebars of the life ladder that I could not see. My mom and I were going through a tough emotional time. Binza and Ravi stood strong, with Lavanya and Shaurya's steadfast support. Our deep link made the word "in-laws" feel inadequate. Because life is so unpredictable, the reader is left guessing what will happen in the next part, which is shrouded in mystery."

Chapter 22
Inspiration comes from Anywhere-

Grab it.

I read a Note from Mr. David Campbell and it inspired me to write it here, with approval- all credit to Mr. David Campbell:

IN TROUBLED TIMES, THERE ARE CHAOS ALL AROUND YOU.

In troubled times the chaos around you need not be reflected inside you. One of the strongest ways to remain on course is to find and know your purpose. There are many ways to combat stress, but the most powerful are associated with feeling secure about who you are and why you were put here. Likewise, feeling that you are on course with your purpose is effective in keeping away anxiety and depression.

Have you been able to find your life's purpose yet? If so, do you feel that you are on track with your purpose? When they first enter the job market, many young people take the best job they can find, and sometimes the only job. There's little or no room to think about something as grand and far-reaching as their purpose in life. But eventually the issue arises. Of all the things that make human beings unique, needing purpose and meaning in our lives is one of the most prominent.

In the tradition of being mentored, your purpose is already waiting for you. It exists at a deeper level of awareness than the mental activity that fills the mind constantly.

The notion that you should find work that brings you bliss and joy is appealing, but Campbell, who had a deep understanding of Eastern spiritual traditions, meant something more. By following your bliss, he contended, "…the life you ought to be living is the one you _are_ living." This holds out a vision that is radically different from the notion that hard work, persistence, and keeping your shoulder to the wheel are the keys to success. As Campbell explained, "Follow your bliss, don't be afraid, and doors will open where you didn't know they were going to be."

At first glance it might seem that he is advising people to jump ship from their current unfulfilling job to grow roses or become an opera singer, but in reality, Campbell was aligning himself with the Indian concept of Dharma. The word derives from a Sanskrit verb that means "to uphold." Your dharma is the way of life supported by the power of pure or cosmic consciousness.

You don't have to believe in either Dharma or "follow your bliss" to experience what countless before you have experienced, namely, that there is a path to finding our purpose that includes many ingredients. Here are the main ones.

· You love your work and feel energized by it.
· You feel that you and the job are a good fit.
· Your surroundings at work are low in stress, pressure, and office politics.
· You contribute something valuable and earn respect for what you do.
· You fulfil some personal ideals, such as being of service, reaching your full potential, or feeling that your work expands your horizons.
· There is an element of creativity in what you do.
· You feel that your co-workers are trustworthy and loyal. The same goes for supervisors and bosses.

These factors will bring you closer to your life's purpose by giving you a purpose today. You don't need to read a crystal ball into the future. Dharma is a path that unfolds in consciousness. By walking it, you discover more and more about yourself, and this brings you closer to a purpose that has evolved with you.

Unfortunately, most people don't see themselves on such a path. They might rate a job according to salary and prestige, for example. Yet the Gallup Organization's polling data strongly suggests that this focus doesn't work. Worldwide Gallup asks people to rate whether they are thriving or merely surviving. Even in prosperous Western societies only about one-third of respondents report that they are thriving.

Thriving isn't measured by your bank account, the size of your house, or how many people work under you. It is measured by your level of well-being. This message is starting to sink in already in many people's lives, particularly in these unsettled times. Campbell was a harbinger of the future, but his advice also echoes centuries past.

At this moment many people want suggestions about returning to their purpose after a time of disruption. Here are some tips.

Don't try to regain lost progress all at once. Begin with activities that are part of your purpose.

A good beginning is to find ways to be of service in small ways with people who are in need.

The key is to feel confident about what you have to give to the world. You can sit down and make a list of your talents and strengths. Then write down one or two ways to use each one in the coming days.

Remember that your purpose isn't the same as your career. Keep your sight fixed on that powerful phrase, "the life you ought to be living." Expand this to include everything that brings you closer to your ideal, and if your career hasn't returned to its previous levels, you can still give of your time, effort, and emotional support to those around you.

Keep your ideals before you. Believe in a higher vision of life and live accordingly. Raise your expectations as high as your ideals. These have been the hallmarks of dharma for millennia, and they hold true today as much, if not more, than ever.

Oscar Wild said – " I am so clever that sometimes I don't understand a single word of what I am being told."

Chapter 23
Accepting the Challenges of Life

Dad left us one terrible morning in Bangalore, and our whole world fell apart. When I found him on the floor, not moving, the sun's soft rays had just touched the horizon. Panic rushed through my body like a wave, making me lose myself in the harsh truth of the situation. As the neighbors quickly called for an ambulance, a sense of desperation filled the air. But time seemed to bend and stretch out into an agonizing eternity.

As we waited for the ambulance's noise to sound far away, my feelings were like a storm. Fear gripped my heart like a vice and wouldn't let go. I felt helpless in the face of the approaching tragedy because I didn't know what would happen. Each second that went by repeated the beating of my heart, a constant reminder of how short life is. I did realize that Mom and me were unwell too.

When the ambulance finally arrived, its loud sirens marked the start of a trip that could not be undone. We got to the hospital in record time, but fate had already taken a life. Dad, who was the rock of our family, had left the lively dance of life. During the ride to the Hospital, Dad briefly opened his eyes and looked at me. That look is something that I have not forgotten even today, 4 years hence. His leaving left a permanent mark on my heart. It was a bittersweet memory of him that made me cry and smile a little.

When I got home, the gap that Dad's absence had left was very clear. But the trials in the universe seemed to never end. Mom bravely fought the last of her breast cancer, but now she is in the cruel grips of Parkinson's and dementia. Our house turned into a safe haven for medical textbooks. Each page told a story of pain and strength.

My sister Binza and her husband Ravi stood out like bright lights in the middle of this storm. Not only did they fly in as a family, but they also stood strong for us. During the difficult process of saying goodbye to Dad, we did the serious last rites that marked the end of an era. Grief weighed heavily on us and made us afraid that the weak bonds that held us together would break.

Binza and Ravi led me to a quiet area in the House and we talked about what had happened. Their eyes showed the same pain I felt, and in that moment of weakness, we both had to face the hard truth that life had dealt us. Though Dad's death was still fresh in our minds, there was an unspoken promise that we would get through this together, drawing power from the love that united us as a family.

Binza's words were like a strong gust of wind that took my breath away. "If you can't take care of yourself, how will you take care of Mom?" The weight of her worry fell heavily on my shoulders. It was a harsh realization that echoed through the silence that followed. The chapter ended quickly, leaving feelings that weren't said hanging in the air and a talk that wasn't finished. It was that moment that we would return to Jabalpur. Smita and Aayush had to stay back, Aayush still a student, and Smita, was the only person who could look for employment in the family. Aayush had also to be taken care of at this crucial juncture of his life.

The decision was taken. Mom and me were going back to Jabalpur.

Going back to Jabalpur, where I was born, was like entering a safe place where I felt at home. I felt better when I was surrounded by people I knew, like School-time classmates, soulmates, and friends. Their presence made me feel safe and warm, like a warm blanket, whispering stories of shared history and unspoken ties. It felt like coming home, a return to the roots that kept me steady in a sea of doubt.

Still, Bangalore cast a dark shadow over our family. The distance was like an unbridgeable chasm, separating us literally but bringing us together in our fight to stay alive. Bangalore continues to be a place, am very hesitant for me to go to again. Go there though.

In Jabalpur, I had to deal with a world that had changed because of my health. Even though I was in a place I knew well, I relied on my inspiration and motivation to reach out and be associated with my life that was built here. Last few months, my support system has been a simple walking stick, which has been with me most of the time. Wasn't totally dependent on the stick, yet another support for me, a Confidence booster, sort of. Every day, I had to take 14 steroids as part of a rite. Each pill was a bitter reminder of how fragile my life was. The life ladder that used to be strong now had side railings, which made me feel like I had assistance from an outside force.

During the quiet times, I thought about what those fences meant to me. Not only were they crutches, but they were also signs of divine guidance. I felt a deep and subtle link to something bigger than myself like I was being blessed from above. These invisible railings became a symbol of the constant support that got me through the storms. They show how strong people can be when they're going through hard times. Each one of us can be.

Every step in the ups and downs of life felt like a careful dance on a tightrope. Even though there were problems, the recognizable faces of Jabalpur were a comfort. In their eyes, I saw understanding, empathy, and the promise that we would make it through this journey together, even though there were a lot of unknowns.

These days, living with my mum is more than just a routine. It's a moving trip where my feelings rise and fall like the tide. The days and nights blend together, making a steady stream of shared times and deep struggles. Showers of blessings come down from everywhere in this emotional battlefield, adding a soft warmth to the tough times.

The people who always help me are my sister Binza, her husband Ravi, and their two children , Lavanya and Shaurya. The word "in-laws" doesn't seem to fully describe how close we are; it goes beyond any legal meaning. Their presence isn't just a formality; it shows that they have a connection that goes beyond social norms. It's a relationship based on love, empathy, and a promise to weather the storms together.

My city, Jabalpur, is a picture with both problems and pleasures. Whenever I take a step, I remember my dad's contagious smile and the strong character he taught me. The walking stick and the daily dose of steroids are constant companions on this unpredictable trip, real-world reminders of how short life is. Even so, the close-knit group of family and friends shines a light of love and support through these tough times.

In the middle of Jabalpur's daily chaos, life is a mosaic of feelings. Mom's problems make up a painful story that I watch unfold, one that is etched with the harsh truth of getting older. Witnessing her fights breaks my heart and makes me question how strong my emotions are. It tests the limits of what I can handle. But even though things are bad, the fact that our family is united brings us comfort and heals the scars that time has caused.

The tough things become manageable because of the love that surrounds us like a shield. Every smile shared and every hand held becomes a lifeline in the storm of feelings. Mom is very unwell, bedridden for a Year, with Dementia, Parkinson's. We find strength in being together as we sail through the rough waters of life. In Jabalpur, where every corner tells a story of the past, our family is what keeps us steady when things go wrong.

In the busy city of Bangalore, Aayush continues to do well, employed by now. He is an inspiration to me and makes me feel good. To us, his accomplishments are a source of joy and proof of how strong our family is. At the same time, Smita continues to work hard. Even though there are miles between us, there are still threads that hold our lives.

The road we're on is not at all smooth. It's a mountain range of ups and downs, a symphony of problems and successes. Still, when I don't know what to do, the side railings of spiritual gifts help me stay on track. As a gentle warning that there is something bigger at work, guiding the unseen forces that shape our lives, they give us a sense of stability.

As this part of my life unfolds, I come to a deep realization: self-care is very important. Binza's words play in my head like a melody, a gentle warning that I need to take care of myself before I can take care of Mom and the family. It's a lesson that I've learned over the years and is a key part of the complex dance of responsibilities that makes up my job. As I start to take care of myself, the help from my extended family is like a lifesaver. When these ties go beyond what the law says they are, they become sources of strength. The understanding and love that flow through these links act as a safety net, giving comfort when life is uncertain.

The emotional tapestry that these relationships have made, is a proof of how strong people are. The real heart of family can be seen in the shared laughs, knowing looks, and body language that isn't said. At these times, the miles between us seem less important, and the way our lives are linked becomes real, like a force that goes beyond space.

As I keep figuring out this complicated web of life, I find comfort in the power of my family, both close and far away. With the help of the spiritual side railings, every step is a deliberate move towards a future where love and self-care are intertwined, weaving a strong fabric that will last. Something like a silver lining in a cloudy sky shows up in the middle of our problems. Moments of happiness, like laughing with people we care about, become our lifelines and help us get through the rough parts of life. Our home city of Jabalpur turns into a symbol of strength when every day is not only a task but also a chance to find our own strength and appreciate the love that surrounds us.

Even though there are hard times in Jabalpur, life is a journey of unwavering drive. Every day bears the weight of lessons learned and the chance to grow even when life is hard. The warmth of shared moments and the sounds of laughter become our guides through the dark times, telling us that even in the worst times, there is a source of joy to be found. As the trip goes on, I take comfort in being thankful for the side rails that help me stay on track. They help me in more ways than one; they are spiritual gifts that keep me going when things get hard. These fences, which I can't see but feel deeply in my soul, remind me that I'm not going through this rough journey by myself.

We're getting blessed like a light rain, and I'm reminded of the special moments that make life worth living. For me, the most important parts of life are the easy things, the shared smiles, and the warm embraces of family. Each blessing is like a lifeline that pulls us out of the depths of sorrow and gives us new hope to keep going.

But the strongest strength may be the unbreakable ties that make up a family. Our family bonds are strong because we share stories, understand each other without saying so, and hold each other through hard times. These connections give us a sense of stability and love that lasts through the hard times we go through.

I'm learning that trouble isn't the end, but the start of something new. It's a chance to live fully, to enjoy a variety of experiences, and to see the delicate beauty that exists even when things are hard. It's a chance to really enjoy what it means to live before we have to say goodbye to this journey, we call life.

"Binu Varghese's life takes a great step ahead, when his old school, St. Aloysius, asks him to lead the School Assembly for EX Students for the Sesquicentennial Celebrations. This happens during the ongoing fight against sarcoidosis. Binu and the people watching are both amazed as the former School Captain plans the event, which mixes elements from the past and the present. Even though Binu is sick, his unwillingness to give up becomes a mantra that runs through the story. The story starts with a moving statement from a person Binu has helped, which starts the "Gratefulness Challenge." Nominating Soumya Padmanabhan adds to the mystery and hints at shocking reveals and unlikely alliances in the next part of Binu's amazing journey. Eager to find out what surprises fate has in store ?"

Chapter 24
Refusing to Die Until I Die

In my ongoing fight against sarcoidosis, I stand firm, like a warrior who will not give up, as this sneaky enemy keeps attacking me. It's a trip with lots of turns and turns, an emotional roller coaster that tests everything about me. Mr. Sarcoidosis has tried to bring me down, like an enemy that won't give up. It has cast a shadow over my spirit. Still, here I am, unwilling to give up. That thing should be hanging its head in failure, but I'm not going to let it. With resolve written all over my body, I speak out against sarcoidosis: "Find another soul to torture, my friend, because I will not give up."

Even though things are hard, there is a music of feelings playing in the background. There are times when everything seems like it could fall on me, but the love and support around me make me strong. Friends and family become the things that hold me up, and their support is like a balm for the cuts that this condition keeps inflicting.

There's a surprising source of happiness in the middle of this rough journey—a bright spot in the darkness. Conducting Training sessions for "People Development, Leadership, Self Confidence, Facing Interviews, Personality Development" training classes gives me a chance to share my knowledge and experience with people who are eager to learn. Helping young people and seeing the understanding on their faces is a bittersweet victory over the bad things that want to take over my life.

St. Aloysius School, where I went to school, puts out its hand to me, which makes my impact even stronger. The school's Principal, Fr. Sibi Joseph, contacts me and asks for me to conduct training Programmes for both Teachers and Students. It makes me feel so nostalgic to go back to the halls where I started my own educational journey, and the fact that they asked me for this Professional assignment, was a great feeling for me. St. Aloysius has grown from one single Branch to 3 more in Jabalpur. Was proud to go back to each of these branches to execute the Training.

As a former student, being able to stand in front of teachers as a guide shows how strong you are. It's not just a workout; it's a journey back to the places that shaped me. Every encounter and shared moment is a stroke on the canvas of my legacy, and I'm proud to be a part of St. Aloysius School's ongoing story.

For the Sesquicentennial, I made a determined and hard bid to gather Ex Aloysians for the special day. One Hundred and Fifty Years of the School – A Birthday, none of us have celebrated, or ever will. The School planned the day, the core committee set up included me and we got into the nitty-gritty of every single minute. Fr. Sibi is a great planner and includes his team for each step to be taken.

When the day arrived, 300 of us landed into School. What an emotional moment, it was reflected in the tepid and enthusiastic Hellos and Hugs. Some delegates were decades apart. When I got a call from Canada and asked for assistance to register, I asked the gentleman, the Year he had passed out from school, a detail required to register the person. His response was-"Binu, when I passed out from School, you were not even born then" !!! Yesterday was meeting Today and Tomorrow, who were smiling.

What an Amazing day spent in the school campus.

St .Aloysius has a legacy of persons who have led the Institution. As Principals of this eminent Institution, they have been outstanding Individuals. For a start, when I was in School, it was Fr. Davis George, my Mentor and Inspiration. Fr. Thankachan Jose stepped in and am amazed at what he did in the rural village of Ghughri, actually farming nature by himself and now as Director of St. Paul's Katni. As I come back now , Fr. Sibi Joseph is here. It is not a job for him. It is a 'Mission'. Notice, how each of them has become an integral part of my life, a student who passed out Thirty-Four (34) YEARS ago !!

When things go wrong, I find meaning. Sarcoidosis is a tough enemy, but my name is Binu Varghese and I'm from Jabalpur. My story is one of strength, resilience, and the unwavering search for a worthwhile life.

I was right in the middle of the celebrations for St. Aloysius' Sesquicentennial Year, which is a tribute to the school's 150 years of wonderful history. It was a happy event that called for me to play a key part in planning it. When I stood in front of the school assembly, I thought back to when I was school captain and felt a rush of feelings. There was more to it than just a party; it was a trip through time that connected the past and the present.

Having participants who had walked these halls decades before I was born added a deep level of meaning to the event. There was a lot of history in the school that could be heard in the halls from the people who had lived there. I stood tall, even though my health problems were heavy on my mind. I wouldn't let them control my future.

Life has been a series of fights, and I have been determined to win every one of them. Even though my health isn't perfect, my spirit is still whole. It's an unstoppable force that won't be tamed. I'm not going through this trip by myself; my family's unwavering support has been my anchor in the rough seas of hardship.

My mother has been there for me through all of my problems. She is a source of love and strength. Her steadfast support has given me strength and comfort, and it has reminded me that there is light even in the darkest times. Mom is fighting her own battles. So unwell that we Pray for Peace for her. .Along with her, my sister Binza and her husband Ravi have been the rock-solid support I've needed to build my strength.

My life is like a complicated fabric, and the threads of family make it strong and united. Lavanya and Shaurya, Binza's children, have grown up to be sources of unwavering strength. Their laughing echoes through my heart, a melody that goes beyond the limits that health puts on us. Because they support me to, I keep doing things that make me happy and give my days meaning, even though my health may be putting limits on me.

The Sesquicentennial Year was more than just a way to remember; it was a sign of how strong the human spirit is. I learned that the celebration wasn't just about the years that had passed, but also about the strength that lasts through the embrace of family and the shared past of St. Aloysius. It was a powerful reminder that life is a beautiful trip that should be enjoyed one moment at a time, even when things go wrong.

During my trip, I've held on to a philosophy that is more than just a way to stay alive; it's about loving life until the very end. It means committing to live with fire and purpose, like a flame that won't go out. In this quest, I've learned how powerfully one life can affect another. This realization came to me through the story of a person I had the honor of mentoring.

The way I inspired this lady taught this person to be grateful moved others, and they were then chosen for the "Gratefulness Challenge," a program I created. Their writings, which came about because of this task, showed how recognizing blessings, even in hard times, can change things. The task made them stop, think, and count their blessings—those small but important things in life that we often forget about in the midst of all the chaos. As they dug deeper, family and friends naturally took the top spots on the thanks pyramid, as they should. Still, among the familiar faces of loved ones, three gifts stood out, and each one made me feel something.

The most valuable gift was health, which is often taken for granted until it breaks. In the tapestry of their thoughts, the threads of gratitude for health and happiness were woven with deep feeling. When they realized that good health, even when it came with problems, was the basis for a happy life, their heart beat faster with thanks.

The next thing on the list was the warmth of love, which came through in their writing. It wasn't just accepted that family and friendship are important; they were praised. It was a powerful reminder that the connections we build are the jewels that make up our lives.

Last but not least, the gift of time stood tall and cast a shadow over their gratitude book. Time, an intangible but important asset, became a light for reflection. Being aware that every moment, laugh, and tear shed with loved ones was a gem in the bank of memories made them value those moments even more.

I saw how a simple task could change people's lives by following their journey of gratitude. It was like a positive wave that went out beyond the surface. I saw the beauty of being strong and resilient in their images. It makes you strong to count your blessings, no matter how small they are.

The "Gratefulness Challenge" was like a thread through the weave of life; it brought people together and made them feel grateful. It made me realize that even when things are hard, being thankful can light up the darkest places and tell us that every breath is a gift and every moment is a chance to live with passion and purpose.

They were thankful for more than just their own successes. They were thankful for all the love and support that made up their lives. Each chance wasn't just a way to get to the next one; it was a sign of the love and faith that was all around them. One could feel the deep feelings that went along with these moments in the way their thoughts echoed: a mix of humility and awe as they recognised how generosity and personal growth are linked.

At the same time they were thanking people, they were also very proud of being "Indian." Their life was full of bright colours that came from the many and varied parts of their culture. Recognition of their roots, even though it was simple, made them feel like they belonged because it connected them to a tradition. Their words showed how proud they were to be part of an Indian culture full of traditions, colours, and stories. This gave a clear picture of how important their Indian identity was to them emotionally.

As the reflective trip came to an end, a moving event happened: Soumya Padmanabhan was chosen for the gratitude challenge. When people spread happiness and thanks, a beautiful chain reaction began. The feelings that went into this action showed how powerful it is to recognise and appreciate someone. It was more than just a nomination; it was a way for them to remember how much they appreciated the kindness shown to them and start a chain of thanks that went beyond their own lives.

As life goes ups and downs, the "Gratefulness Challenge" shows up as a soft whisper, reminding us that even in the hardest times, gratitude can be our guide light. It's a call to recognise the unwavering support of those we love, who quietly help us win. When we take time to think about the hard things we've been through, our feelings rise like a tide. The warmth of thanks covers the scars of our past problems.

Each entry in a gratitude diary is like a chapter in a story about how different experiences have changed us. These are not just stops along the way; they are important landmarks on the path to mental growth and strength.

At its core, this story isn't just about surviving; it's a dance of living and making a difference. The inner core is the search for a life that goes beyond just existing. A positive memory that spreads through other people's lives is what it means to leave an indelible mark on the world. The challenge makes you think, and when you do, you realize that the most important thing in life is the effect you make, no matter how big or small.

Here I am, Binu Varghese from Jabalpur, a strong person who doesn't give up when life gets hard. The problems may cast their shades, but I will not give up until the very end. Along this trip, feelings weave through my story like a tapestry, showing how strong the human spirit is.

"In the middle of chaos, I discover a deep truth: having a purpose protects you from inner turmoil during hard times. I dealt with the ups

and downs of life and eventually learned about the ancient idea of Dharma. This is more than just looking for happiness; it's a dance with the world. There are signs that point to a meaningful life, such as a love of work, a perfect job fit, and a stress-free workplace. Binu's journey turns into a search for self, which fits with how the idea of meaning changes over time. The story questions common ways of measuring success and gives advice on how to find meaning again when things are going wrong. It tells Binu to start small, help others, and think about more than just their job. Look att what happens in the next exciting part of this deep journey towards purpose and meaning."

Chapter 25
Walking Your Path to Purpose

In the stormy seas of life, rough waves crash all around us, threatening to swallow us up in chaos. Still, in the middle of the storm, there is a stronghold where our feelings can find safety. Getting around in these crazy times is like using a compass, which stays true even when things are going crazy around you. This guide, our lighthouse, points straight towards a goal, a North Star that lights the way through the darkness. While the trip is hard, knowing that we are moving towards something important makes it easier to handle.

Imagine being at a point where you don't know what to do next. Every step feels like a jump into the unknown. It is at these times that our feelings become very important, adding bright colours to the story of our trip. Think about the fear that fills your heart as you take your first steps into the working world. You could get lost in the job market, which is like an unpredictable sea. In your haste to stay stable, you might jump at the first chance that comes your way. That's just how we're wired to respond to the urgent need for security.

When we first start working, thinking about the big picture of our lives may seem like a luxury, something far away that we can't focus on because of our bills and other tasks. While the story keeps going, the plot gets more complicated, and the search for meaning becomes a main theme. Realising that meaning isn't a silly pursuit but an important part of what makes us human is a turning point. It's the thing that makes us unique.

As you go through this journey, think about the emotional landscape. Imagine how frustrating it is to have a job that doesn't seem to fit with your goals; a painful dissonance that echoes through your daily life. It's possible that the weight of unrealized potential casts a shadow over your efforts. But even in this dark time, the search for meaning can inspire you.

As you look for your life's meaning, picture the clear moments as sunlight breaking through storm clouds. These events, which are emotional and life-changing, become the steps towards harmony. You can't just get to the goal of finding your meaning; you have to go on a journey that requires you to be strong, think deeply, and always strive for authenticity.

Have you found your North Star yet? Do you sense that your purpose is pulling you through the maze of life? Allow yourself to feel the emotions that are woven into this story, because that's how the real meaning of the trip comes out.

There is a purpose waiting for you deep inside, gently whispering advice to you like a wise teacher from a place of deep awareness. It calls you beyond the constant chatter in your thoughts, with a voice that goes beyond the everyday.

Just think about the idea of finding joy in your work—what a nice thought. However, Joseph Campbell, a wise man who knows a lot about Eastern spiritual practices, wants us to go deeper and understand things more fully. Following your bliss isn't just about being happy on the surface; it's also about finding the way to live your life that fits with who you really are. It's more than just hard work; it's a personal dance with a reason.

Picture the situation where you go on a trip to find your mission. And it's not just a job; it's a spiritual journey that goes deep into your being. During this trip, your feelings are like bright paints that you use to paint the picture of your experience. As you step into the unknown, you feel a rush of anticipation, like when you see an old friend after never seeing them in years.

As you go through life's maze, picture how you'll feel when you come across a job that sparks something inside you. Not just a short-lived happiness; it's a glimpse of your meaning, a realisation that runs through your whole being. As you get closer to your real calling, the emotional texture gets richer. An inner melody fits in with the beat of your life.

You can feel Joseph Campbell's wisdom as you dive into the deep truth of "Follow your bliss." Letting go of fear leaves you open to being hurt, and having the courage to go after what makes you happy is an emotional release. When doors unexpectedly and by chance open, they carry an emotional weight—a mix of shock and thanks for the coincidences that happen.

Each step you take to get in line with your goal is like a thread in the tapestry of life. The desire to follow your bliss, even when things get hard, adds another level of resolve to the story. As you realise that meaning isn't someplace far away, but a force that's alive and present inside you, your emotions rise to a peak.

So, as you go through life's waves, let your feelings be the compass that points you towards your waiting mission. As you follow your bliss, may you not only find a job but also a deep connection with the life you were meant to live.

In the wise words of Joseph Campbell, the thought of changing careers might seem as silly as growing roses or aspiring to be an opera singer. But below the surface, he talks about a deep idea called Dharma, which has its roots in old Indian philosophy. Dharma, which means "to uphold," is more than just a change in career; it's a way of life that resonates with pure cosmic awareness.

Imagine how deeply you would feel if you accepted Dharma, which is a call to live a meaningful life that goes beyond the everyday. It's like finding a light inside that points you in the direction of a life that is in line with your true self. The idea of Dharma makes people feel revered and connected to a higher cause that makes them want to give their all.

As you go deeper into the world of Dharma, your feelings become the paint that you use to paint this huge picture. Imagine the happiness and satisfaction that come from being in line with a purpose that goes beyond the surface, one that is filled with love, talent, and a sense of making a difference. There are threads of passion, purpose, and a harmonious link to the cosmic symphony of life that run through the emotional tapestry of Dharma.

You don't have to believe in Dharma or "follow your bliss" to know that finding your purpose involves different ingredients. Here are the main ones:

1. Love for Your Work: Your job should energize you.

2. Fit with the Job: You and your job should be a good match.

3. Low Stress and Pressure: A peaceful work environment.

4. Valuable Contribution: You should contribute something important and earn respect.

5. Personal Ideals: Your work should fulfill personal ideals, like being of service or reaching your potential.

6. Creativity: Your work should have a creative aspect.

7. Trustworthy Relationships: Trust among co-workers, supervisors, and bosses.

As you look for your life's purpose, certain events can help you reach important emotional stages that allow your purpose to grow in the present. It's not about looking into a crystal ball to see what will happen in the future. Instead, it's about how Dharma unfolds in your mind. Each step on this path is a revelation, a mirror that shows you deeper parts of yourself and brings you closer to a mission that changes and grows with you.

Think about how you'll feel when you see the signs on this important trip. Like finding puzzle parts that fit together perfectly. It gives you a sense of alignment that makes you happy. Each thing acts as a stepping stone, adding to the mental landscape of the present, which is purposefully woven together.

But not everyone thinks they are on this meaningful road. A lot of people may only look at the pay and prestige of a job and not think about the emotional wealth that comes from being truly satisfied with your work. Think about the emotional distance that happens when seeking outward markers is more important than finding happiness within yourself. It's a small but important change that makes the core of thriving less clear.

Think about how polls around the world that show only about one-third of people in wealthy Western countries feel they are thriving make you feel. Even though most people are constantly trying to be successful in the outside world, the inner void still exists. People all over the world want something more, a deeper sense of meaning that goes beyond material things.

As you go through these emotional waves, think about how much better things would be if you knew you were currently in line with your mission. It's not just a place you want to get to; it's a trip that will help you learn about yourself and feel emotionally fulfilled. Many things make up the emotional tapestry of purposeful living. These include loving your job, being a good fit for it, working in a low-stress environment, making a useful contribution, having personal ideals, being creative, and having trustworthy relationships. Ahead of this, at the Centre of this, and even Behind this- It's about the people who partner with you in Life's journey. I have learned that it is all about People. 'Persons', if I may highlight so. The rich collection of persons who I have been Blessed with, makes living worth it.

True flourishing goes beyond things like money, space in the home, and the number of workers. It has to do with well-being, which is a deep idea that becomes more important during times of change. Joseph Campbell's advice has been around for a long time, but throughout the years it has become more relevant and emotional.

Think about how you'll feel when you understand what living is all about. Having a lot of stuff doesn't mean you're happy; it means you're truly satisfied with your life. Imagine how light your emotional load will be when you put your own needs ahead of social norms and find comfort in the simplicity of a balanced and satisfying life.

Wisdom is to have a mechanism of getting habituated to a gentle reminder to yourself, amidst the noise of societal pressures as it echoes through the halls of time. It's an emotional message to look inside yourself, to change how you measure success, and to find meaning in the deeper, quieter parts of life.

For those trying to find their purpose after disruptions, here are some things Binu has learned:

1. Take Small Steps: Don't try to recover all at once. Start with activities connected to your purpose.

2. Serve Others: Help those in need in small ways. It's a good beginning.

3. Identify Your Strengths: List your talents and strengths. Find ways to use each in the coming days.

4. Purpose vs. Career: Remember, your purpose isn't the same as your career. Focus on living "the life you ought to be living."

5. Keep Your Ideals High: Believe in a higher vision of life. Live by your ideals. Your expectations should match your ideals.

These timeless pieces of advice come from personal experience and Sarcoidosis has been a boulder on the path. Helping me to tell my own story. They still have an emotional power that makes them more relevant today. Imagine how you'll feel when you accept these timeless traits—it's like feeling the comforting embrace of ancient wisdom, a hand on your shoulder as you manage the complicated world of today.

As you go along your own unique road, think about how it will make you feel to know that your purpose isn't a faraway goal but a journey that is always unfolding. It's not just a place you want to go; it's the emotional beat of every step you take. Think about the different feelings that go along with this journey: the excitement of finding something new, the happiness of being in the right place, and the quiet satisfaction that comes with each step towards success.

In a world where life moves quickly, these timeless tips become emotional anchors that keep you stable in the face of all the change. Not only do they give you direction, but they also whisper to you, reassuring you that your journey has value. Take these ideas to heart, and let the emotional tapestry of purpose work itself into every beat of your heart and step you take on this deep journey.

Robert Frost said: *'The woods were lovely, dark, and deep, and I had Miles to go before I slept'*.

Na, that is not what Robert Frost said.

He said: "The woods are lovely, dark, and deep, and I have Miles to go before I sleep".

www.ingramcontent.com/pod-product-compliance
Lightning Source LLC
LaVergne TN
LVHW061342080526
838199LV00093B/6917